LIVE
YOUR
LIFE

14 DAYS TO THE BEST YOU

Ann L. LeFevre, PhD, LCSW, CMT

Disclaimer

The material in this publication is intended for educational purposes only, to assist readers in creating their best lives. This book is not intended to be a substitute for the advice of licensed medical or mental health providers. Readers should consult with their providers on any health-related matters. The author assumes no responsibility for any outcome from the application of the material in this book.

Paperback ISBN: 978-0-9992687-0-4

Digital ISBN: 978-0-9992687-1-1

Interior Design: Christina Gorchos, 3CsBooks.com

Editor: Amy Teegan, LemonandRaspberry.com

DEDICATION

I dedicate this book to my wife, Kieu,
who introduced me to coffee at the perfect time…
right when I started writing this book.

CONTENTS

ACKNOWLEDGMENTS

THANK YOU FIRST AND FOREMOST TO MY FAMILY, including my wife, mother, sister and son. You always support me, no matter how crazy my ideas sound. Thank you to my friends for encouraging me throughout the writing of this book, and a very special word of appreciation to Jen, who offered to read my draft and give some feedback, and who came through in a big way. Thank you!! Much appreciation to Honoree Corder, who inspired me with her book, You Must Write a Book. Turns out she was right! Finally, thank you to my readers. Your time is a gift that I don't take for granted.

INTRODUCTION

I'M GLAD YOU DECIDED TO READ THIS BOOK! There is so much waiting for you in your best life, and I'm excited for you to start your journey. If you've been feeling dissatisfied with your current circumstances, chronically stressed or burned out, or you've been wanting to make changes but need some guidance, then you've come to the right place. In this program, you will be guided to identify sources of dissatisfaction, learn how to address them quickly and easily, and move forward to live your best life. My purpose in writing this book is simple – I want to remind you of things you already know but may have forgotten, teach you some new skills, encourage you to find the strength and commitment to make changes where needed, and walk beside you as you make this amazing journey. Along the way, I believe you will find contentment, satisfaction, motivation, desire and passion, and genuine excitement for your life.

I know how valuable your time is, and I don't want to waste one single minute of it. With that in mind, I designed this book to quickly bring you the results you want. Each day includes a lesson that has been successfully used by my clients over the years, illustrated with stories from my own life. The chapters conclude with lists of "Thinking Points" and "Action Items," which will help you personalize the lesson and apply it to your life. I've seen many lives change through the application of these time-tested tips, and I'm certain they will help you too.

To get the full benefit of this book, please download and print the free companion workbook I've created just for you at www.restorebodyandsoul.com/books. This workbook will provide structure as you're completing the Action Items, while giving you extra space to jot down your thoughts and ideas as you go. If you prefer to use your own journal instead, that is totally fine, but please do write down your ideas and thoughts each day. I am confident you will undergo a transformation over the course of this book, and the more effort and energy you put into this process, the more you will benefit and the better outcomes you'll see.

This book is separated into fourteen "days," but please look at each day as a chapter or a lesson that does not have a specific time limit. You can take as long as you need to read and reflect on each one. You may find that one lesson really clicks with you, and you want to take an entire week and apply it wholeheartedly to your life. That's totally fine! Another chapter may not be as meaningful to you right now, and you'll choose to read it through quickly and move along to the next one. No problem! I do encourage you to read every chapter, even if the title doesn't immediately grab your attention. The titles don't fully represent the depth of the material being presented; I purposely created them to be very simple because I want you to remember them. I have a feeling that the lesson names will start popping into your head at times when you are faced with the opportunity to apply them.

I want to make an important point here, to be clear right from the start. This is not a book about finding happiness or creating a happy life for yourself. Happiness is a somewhat mythical experience, in my opinion. A short-lived "high" that passes faster than a cloud in the sky. No doubt you will find moments of happiness as you go on this journey, and that's wonderful. However, when the high fades, as it always does, please carry on. You are going to create a life that is meaningful to you, a life of value that you will find satisfying and enriching, and that is more important than seeking brief, elusive moments of happiness.

As you're making your way, you will be challenged, and you may feel uncomfortable or a little frustrated as you try new things. Please stick with it and keep reminding yourself to trust the process. Creating the best you involves finding out what works for you, and also what isn't helpful right now. Not succeeding at something is NOT the same as failing. If something doesn't work out as you intended, look at it as data. It's just information that helps you learn more about yourself. Think of yourself as a researcher, someone who is becoming an expert on YOU and what works for you. Researchers must collect a lot of data before drawing any conclusions, and the data is never 100% what they were expecting. Just gather the information, and learn from it so you don't have to keep collecting that same piece of data.

Before we begin, I want to briefly introduce myself, to give you a glimpse at my background and the foundation of my perspectives and world views. I am a PhD, Licensed Clinical Social Worker (LCSW), and I've been working as a psychotherapist since 2001. I am also a Certified Massage Therapist (CMT) and a Certified Acupressurist. I work full-time as a clinical social worker and manager in a mental health clinic, while also growing a health and wellness enterprise that I feel quite passionate about called Restore Body and Soul. At Restore Body and Soul, I integrate time-tested Eastern and evidence-based Western treatment techniques, with a focus on the mind-body connection. I provide massage therapy, psychotherapy, workshops and classes on acupressure and other health and wellness topics, personal and professional consultation, and I also personally make and sell all-natural bath and body products designed with relaxation and restoration in mind. You can check out my website at www.restorebodyandsoul.com if you'd like to learn more about my offerings.

Some people think it's strange, being both a clinical social worker and a massage therapist, but it makes sense to me. Since my childhood years, I've known that my purpose in life is to serve others, to help others feel better, to work with others and help them have the best lives they possibly can with the resources they're given. While working with my clients from the social work perspective, I quickly learned that we cannot separate the mind from the body. Our memories are stored in our brains AND in our muscles, organs and cells. Our emotions may stem from the brain, yet our anger is armor, our anxiety is butterflies, and our depression is the weight of the world. While it is incredibly therapeutic to mentally examine thought patterns and related emotions, it is also important to physically ease the tension and blocked energy that is stored in the body as the result of those thought patterns and connected memories. I think it's vital to treat the whole person, so for me, being a social worker and a massage therapist is only natural.

Okay, it's almost time! Before we jump into Day 1, please grab your companion workbook and open to the first page. Right now, think about your life and how you're feeling about your life, situation, circumstances, your overall "life satisfaction." On a scale of 1-10, with 1 being "my life is in the toilet right now" and 10 being "my life is AMAZING and I'm completely satisfied," what number would you give your life? Please don't rush through this. Take your time and think about how you feel about yourself and your life when you wake up in the morning, and when you're getting ready for bed at night. Think about your daily and weekly routines and how you spend your time. How satisfied are you? Write down your number. We'll revisit this at the end.

To prepare yourself for Day 1, and prior to starting your reading each day, I'd like you to take a few minutes to ground yourself. It's important to ground or center yourself each day before you pick up this book. No doubt you were busy doing something or thinking about something right before you sat down to read, and I want you to be ready, relaxed and fully present, each time you approach this material. Go ahead and roll your shoulders frontwards a few times, and then backwards a few times. Turn your head gently from side to side, then up and down. Stretch your arms up over your head, then back down again. Gently but vigorously shake out your hands and feet. Finish with several slow, deep breaths. (You can view this brief grounding exercise at www.restorebodyandsoul.com/books).

Let's get started!

DAY 1

SILENCE
THE VOICES

GROWING UP, I WAS NEVER MUCH OF AN athlete. I grew up in the woods, in the heart of nature, with opportunities to hike and climb and play, but I preferred to read and play piano. If my family went for a hike or a vacation that required some walking, I would always whine and need to sit down and "take a break." I wasn't completely sedentary when I was little, however. I got some physical activity when I would pretend to be a dancer or singer in my basement. But as a young child, I don't think anyone would have described me as "active".

When I was six years old and in the first grade, I had a gym teacher – let's call her Mrs. Z. She was not soft and friendly like my classroom teacher, and her communication style was to bark directions and yell louder when she thought we weren't doing something right. Mrs. Z was intimidating to the first grade me, and I hated when she yelled.

Looking back, I wonder if she didn't like her job, or maybe she was burned out. Who knows, maybe she was just a jerk. I've learned that you can't make excuses for everyone.

In the late spring of that year, we were training for the annual track and field day. We didn't have a track at my elementary school, so we ran a loop around the perimeter of one of the grassy fields behind the playground. Sometimes we practiced running one time around the loop and aimed for speed. Other times we had to run a few times around and aimed for endurance. We sometimes ran a relay where we passed a baton to the person who was running next in line, which took teamwork and coordination. Then there was a small sprinting area, and even a place set up where we had to jump as far as we could.

It was hot. Track and field day was always at the end of the school year, right at the time when the temperature was starting to soar. I quickly realized, at age 6, that running a loop in a grassy field in the middle of the day while the sun beat down on me wasn't much fun. I didn't like to sweat, and I really didn't like to exert that much energy. I learned that I didn't enjoy running for sport, and none of this was very fun at all.

Nevertheless, I did my best. I was raised to excel, to give my all at everything I did. For example, I had started playing piano at age 3, and I was reading above my grade level from the time I started school. I knew how to push myself. I wasn't a natural athlete, and I wasn't instinctively competitive, but I had the drive to be the very best I could be, so I ran to the best of my ability in the hot sun because that's who I was.

One particularly hot, sunny day in gym class, I was running around that God-forsaken loop, the loop I had come to dread. I was sweating and thirsty, but I kept putting one foot in front of the other, knowing I would eventually finish. I was coming down a straightaway, when Mrs. Z pulled me over to the side. I thought that was strange, but I was willing to take a quick break. She looked me in the eye, and barked, "What if you played piano the way you run? What would your piano teacher say?"

Did I mention that I was a sensitive child? Well, I was a sensitive child, and I wasn't used to being yelled at or criticized by teachers. I stood there and looked at Mrs. Z, dumbfounded. I was also a shy and quiet child (except at home), and I mumbled something along the lines of, "I don't know," and then went back to the loop to continue running.

When I got home, I told my mom what had happened. My mom was livid, and yes, she called the school. This teacher had pulled me aside and criticized me in a very direct and personal way, which was not okay. My mom may have gone in there in person and met with my teacher or the principal or Mrs. Z personally, I really don't remember. Knowing my mom, she probably did. But the damage was done.

At age 6, I believed my teachers were the smartest people in the world. They were teachers, for heaven's sake, which meant they were experts who knew everything about everything. If my gym teacher thought I was a lousy runner, then I was a lousy runner. In fact, if I was a lousy runner, I was probably lousy at all sports. If I was lousy at all sports, I shouldn't even try to do them because I would only bring shame to myself and the team. In fact, I should stay to the back in gym class, and skip four-square and dodgeball at recess. I was never going to be an athlete, and if I tried, others would criticize me and I'd feel embarrassed.

Wow. See how quickly a young child can take one criticism, and internalize it into a life-altering core belief? I don't remember if Mrs. Z ever apologized to me. I doubt it, because that's not the kind of person she was and she probably forgot about that comment as soon as she said it. But it changed the way I saw myself, from that moment on. I was embarrassed about my self-perceived lack of athletic ability, and I never joined a sports team or club during my time in school. It's possible that I would've never joined anyway, because like I said, I didn't really enjoy challenging myself physically, but who knows?

When I look back, I wonder, what if Mrs. Z would have instead called me over and said, "Ann, I can see that you are hot and this is not very fun, but great job for pushing yourself anyway and giving your all. Keep going!" Would my life, at least in terms of my choices to play or not play sports, and my way of thinking about my athletic abilities have been different? Would I have had more body confidence growing up, and maybe felt better about myself overall?

Words matter. They matter to everyone, and especially to young children. It took me decades to get to the point where I could recognize the damage that was done to my young self's confidence that day, training for track and field in the hot sun at my elementary school. I can't say that I ever thought specifically about Mrs. Z over the years, or blamed her for my lack of physical or athletic confidence…I never actually thought about her again until much later in life. But as an adult, I realize the impact of her words on the young me, and I'm thankful that I was eventually able to say, "Screw you, Mrs. Z. Your words are no longer part of me. I am strong enough and fast enough, and I always have been."

SILENCE THE VOICES

Do you hear negative voices in your head, trying to convince you that you're not good enough, strong enough, smart enough, pretty or handsome enough, thin enough, fit enough, _____ enough? Silence the voices. Those voices are not telling you YOUR truth. They are not serving any purpose except to limit you.

The next time you notice a voice in your head trying to tell you that you are not _____ enough, stop whatever it is you're doing. Turn your head and look in a different direction, and say the opposite to yourself, "I am (blank) enough." I am good enough, fast enough, fit enough, whatever enough. If you're alone, say it out loud. Try doing this immediately, at the first whispers of that negative voice. You may feel silly at first, and you probably won't believe what you're saying if you've been listening to that negative voice for years, but continue to practice. This is a very powerful exercise that may need to be repeated many times a day or even several times an hour. Silencing those voices, taking away their power, will change your life.

There are times when I still hear negative voices. For example, if I have a rough day at work and I feel like I didn't do something well enough, I leave feeling down on myself, and I'm inclined to tell myself negative things about everything I should've done better. But, I no longer get sucked in and let that negative voice dominate the rest of my evening. Instead, I've learned to look at my day, my actions, and my choices from a distance, which is sometimes called the "helicopter view."

If someone were in a helicopter looking down on me and my life right now, would my concerns and issues look like a big deal to them? From the helicopter view, did I really mess up that badly, or was I perhaps exaggerating or dwelling on things that weren't that important?

One hundred percent of the time, after taking the helicopter view, I realize that things are never really as bad as I initially thought. And, even if I did make a mistake or a wrong decision, that doesn't make me a bad person. It just makes me human.

The next time you leave work or school or anywhere feeling crappy about yourself, try looking at your day from the helicopter view. I believe you will be surprised at how many negative things got blown out of proportion, out of habit. Silence the voices.

As you silence the negative voices, try to replace them with self-affirmations. There is power in saying self-affirmations. Life-changing power. A self-affirmation can be about your values, what's meaningful to you, or your personal assets. It can also be related to something that you are doing, working on, or becoming. Say it in the present tense, even if you are not quite there in reality. Your brain will hear you and believe you.

Please note, there is some controversy over whether self-affirmations work, and you can read lots of material from the different perspectives. I personally didn't "believe" in self-affirmations, even though I taught clients how to use them, until I started seeing my clients making significant progress on their treatment goals while using them. So, I tried self-affirmations, and I immediately felt more confident, competent, and focused. Call them what you like, but please don't write them off until you really try them.

So what do my self-affirmations look like? When I drive to work in the mornings, I turn off the radio, and say my affirmations out loud. For example, I say that I am strong and confident, smart and skilled at what I do, that I'm healthy and excited to make good choices for my body today, that others enjoy being around my positive energy, and that I am making a difference in the world. The themes of my affirmations vary, depending on what I'm going through, or if I'm facing a challenge.

When I started writing this book, the negative voices in my head tried to stop me even before I got started. I immediately used my self-affirmations to include saying things out loud like, "I am a best-selling author. My books will reach many people and help them change their lives." I felt silly at first, saying these things out loud. To be completely honest, the first time I attempted an author-related affirmation, I only made it half-way through, then I blushed, looked around my empty car, and immediately started laughing at my dramatic reaction to an affirmation. And then I tried it again, and again.

Saying those self-affirmations was hard for me, because I had barely started writing my first book. However, it didn't matter if they were "true," because that wasn't the point. Saying those affirmations each day, the entire time I wrote this book, gave me the confidence I needed to carry on and finish. Self-affirmations are incredibly powerful. Please don't let a feeling of silliness stop you from trying them. Silence the voices.

THINKING POINTS:

- Did anyone ever tell you that you couldn't or shouldn't do something? That you weren't good enough, fast enough, pretty enough, _____ enough?

- Or, were those notions implied through limitations that were placed on you or opportunities that passed over you?

- When an opportunity comes your way, do you automatically think that you can't or shouldn't do it, and then you list all the reasons why you shouldn't do it? Do you find yourself listing the same reasons over and over?

- When you have a rough day, do those negative feelings carry over into your evening and even the next day?

ACTION ITEMS:

- The next time a negative voice from your past, or a negative automatic thought comes up for you, literally turn your head to look in the opposite direction, and say the opposite to yourself, out loud if possible. Write down the opposite statement in your workbook, even if you don't believe it yet. You may have believed this voice for a long time, but it's not your truth any longer. Keep doing this, every time this same thought tries to sneak its way back into your mind.

- When you have a difficult day and the negative voices are overwhelming, try adopting a helicopter view. Look at your day, your situation, and your circumstances from a distance, and ask yourself if what happened is really all that significant. Keep doing this exercise, and you will learn how to quickly get perspective and silence the voices.

- Start writing and saying self-affirmations on what is meaningful and valuable to you, what you represent, and what you want to do or are in the process of doing. I personally find it helpful to say a combination of statements that are currently true (e.g., "I am kind, I am enough as I am") and statements that I'm working towards ("I am a best-selling author," or "I can complete a 5k race"). Our brains believe what we tell it, so say these affirmations confidently and consistently for the best results. Say them when you're getting ready for your day, and even at the end of your day right before you fall asleep. You might feel silly the first time, but by the second time you'll be able to say them loud and clear.

DAY 2

STAY
THE COURSE

EARLIER THIS YEAR, I SIGNED UP FOR LESLIE Sansone's 100-day walking challenge. If you're not familiar with Leslie, she is a fitness expert who created the "Walk at Home" program many years ago. Her indoor walks are accessible to people of any age and fitness level, and I just love her and her workouts. I wasn't familiar with her walking challenge, and I was very excited to receive her email inviting me to join.

I tend to get bored quickly with workouts, and I was at the point where I needed something new. This challenge sounded perfect for me, plus my workouts would be covered for the next few months! The deal was, participants needed to walk one mile every single day for 100 days. You could certainly walk more than one mile, but any extra miles only counted for the day you walked them. You couldn't build up walking credits and pay off mileage deficits.

One hundred days may not sound like a very long time, but when you commit to doing anything every day for 100 days, that's a serious commitment. Especially if it means setting aside time each day to change clothes, lace up sneakers and potentially sweat.

I started the challenge by completing the mandatory one mile each day, and adding an extra mile here and there. There was the occasional day when I walked the mile using one of Leslie's walking DVDs, but the large majority of walks were taken outside. I averaged a 20-minute mile and I was satisfied with myself. I wasn't seeing any changes in my body, but the challenge wasn't to lose a certain amount of weight or really change physically at all; it was simply to walk one mile a day for 100 days. I was doing great, keeping steady and committed.

After completing the first month, I started getting a little bored, so I gradually added more distance. While my goal remained one mile each day, and I was still satisfied with one mile if there was a day I was very busy or feeling under the weather, my average grew to two miles each day. You know what I noticed? It was STILL BORING! There were only so many ways to walk around the neighborhood, for heaven's sake.

One evening, my wife was walking with me, and about halfway into our walk, out of the blue I said, "let's run to the stop sign up ahead...1, 2, 3, go." A new routine of "boosting" was born, similar to the boosts that Leslie uses in her walking videos. We would walk, and then I would say "moderate boost to the speed bump, 1, 2, 3, go," or "fast boost to the light pole, go." We would walk maybe half a block, and then boost another quarter of the block. I felt exhilarated, excited, and lighthearted after that first night of adding running to my routine. I couldn't wait for the next day to try it again.

Unfortunately, I have longstanding knee issues, dating back to my college years. I can usually get away with running for a few days, and then I get severe knee pain that forces me to stop. I had a feeling the same thing would happen this time, but I really wanted it to last because the boosts were so fun. Mind you, I was slower than molasses, but it didn't matter. I was enjoying myself and doing something healthy for my heart and my muscles.

Well, my knees did start hurting. Not the severe pain that had always forced me to stop, but a strange kind of compression-like pain that is hard for me to describe. And, I kept going. Every single day, I continued to run and walk, even though some days my boosts were the same pace or even slower than the walking portions. And, my knees actually ached all day long, with every single step I took.

At work, when I got up from my desk to walk to the restroom, or to walk from my car to my office, my poor knees hurt and I thought I was going to be forced to stop. However, it was still not the severe pain that had plagued me in the past, so I kept telling myself to take it one day at a time, to push through and persevere.

You know what happened? The pain went away, after maybe 2-3 weeks of discomfort and semi-suffering, and I didn't miss a single day of walking. I was so happy the day my pain was officially gone. There's a certain joy that comes from being pain free after several weeks of suffering, and I didn't take my recovered knees for granted.

I really committed to my boosts, lifting my legs when I ran in true track and field style. I increased the lengths of my boosts, even to the point where I started feeling like I could almost call myself a runner. How crazy was that? Me, the one who doesn't enjoy physical activity, who has bad knees, a runner? Yes!!

I continued doing two miles a day for several more weeks, and I started to notice some changes in my body and mind. I lost a solid 5 pounds, I felt confident when I was outside running and even passing people who were going slower, and I noticed that my posture and overall energy level had improved.

During Week 11 I kept feeling the internal nudge to increase to 3 miles a day, and I started thinking about a route that would add another mile. Week 12, I increased to 3 miles a day for just a few days, and I only walked the third mile, while continuing to boost the first two miles.

You know what the hardest mile was? That darn third mile! I learned that I got bored with just walking, but the boosts added fun and challenge and made the time fly by. However, keeping my potentially "bad knees" in mind, I wanted to get my body used to doing 3 miles before I added more boosts. It was frustrating, to have an exhilarating boosted walk for 2 miles and then a boring third mile. But, I was determined to keep my body healthy, and I had success with adding challenges gradually during the past few months, so I was just going to keep doing what was already working.

I successfully completed the 100-day walking challenge, and I was so proud of myself, recording my total mileage on the last day. Over the course of 100 days, life happens. Sickness, pain, stress from work, issues with kids or family members…the world did not stop turning just because I was completing a challenge.

There were some days when I only walked one mile with no boosts. When I was sick, when my knees were hurting too badly, when I was exhausted…those were the hardest days of all. But I still did it, and I felt good about myself for sticking with it even when it was a struggle.

At the end, I realized that the purpose of committing to walk one mile each day was not to get in shape. Instead, I made a commitment to prioritize time for myself each day, for my own health and fitness. I learned that no matter what happens, I can and will take at least fifteen minutes each day to walk, breathe and take care of myself.

STAY THE COURSE

It's not hard to make a commitment, but it is hard to stick to it. Have you ever committed to a health goal, only to have life get in the way? You commit to a diet, and then the next week your co-worker brings in donuts, your kid begs you to make cookies, and you eat out three times because your schedule was too busy to cook at home? Or, you commit to going to the gym five days a week, and then you pull a muscle or get a stomach bug? It can be very difficult to achieve a goal if your initial commitment is too demanding. Start small, very small, and then stay the course, no matter what.

If I had scoffed at the notion of only walking one mile each day, and set out with a personal agenda to walk 5 miles a day right off the bat (which is 10,000 steps, a common goal set by folks wearing fitness trackers), the outcome would have likely been much different. I've tried jumping in with both feet on fitness goals in the past, and I know myself.

Previously, I tried running a couple miles on Days 1 and 2, and by Day 3 I was in excruciating pain, lying on the sofa with ice on my knees, and that was the end of that. I've tried committing to going to the gym six days a week…I don't think that commitment even lasted through the first week. I committed to attending hot yoga five days a week…nope, didn't even finish the first five days.

The difference with this 100-day challenge, was setting the personal goal to stay the course. No matter what obstacles came up in my life, whether fatigue, feeling overworked or overwhelmed, being sick, having rain, high winds, or a heatwave, I had to show up every day. Walk one mile each day no matter what. My body and brain naturally added challenges along the way for me, and I never had to force anything. I didn't make any sudden increases in length or effort, nor did I put any unnecessary pressure on myself to do anything other than complete one mile each day.

You know what I learned? There's value in setting a slow and steady goal, and fully committing to it. There were some evenings that were so windy and chilly, that I was running with my hood up, tied tightly under my chin, and I still needed to hold my hands over my ears to keep them warm. Other days I was so tired, and all I wanted to do was soak in a bath or read in bed. Regardless, I stayed the course.

When I hit Day 85 of the walking challenge, I was surprised to find myself feeling a little sad and anxious, and I started wondering what I was going to do once the challenge was over. Those daily walks, along with tracking my progress on my challenge sheets, had become part of my regular routine. I was feeling good, and I worried that I would lose my motivation once the challenge was over.

At the end of the challenge, it was clear to me that I needed motivation, accountability, and a new challenge, to keep moving forward. And, the challenge needed to be realistic, doable, and nothing too extreme. My wife suggested signing up for a 5k race, and then training for it. I considered it, and I agreed that training for a 5k race is perfect for my next challenge.

I haven't signed up for a race yet, but I downloaded a 5k training app, and I've been consistent with the workouts. In fact, I'm really loving the training, and once I get through the first few weeks of training, I'm planning to register for my first 5k.

I will stay the course, no matter what.

THINKING POINTS:

- Is there something in your life that you've been wanting to do?

- Are you currently contemplating a goal or activity, but you're just not sure?

- Do you need a new challenge in your life, something that will give you some motivation, excitement and fun?

- Have you set out to reach a similar goal before but burned out almost immediately?

ACTION ITEMS:

- Choose one thing you'd like to work on. It could be exercise, diet, developing a journaling habit, cleaning out a garage or closet, learning how to build or create something, learning a sport, hobby or craft, or how to cook or bake. Your options are endless!

- Set a goal for yourself, a goal that feels very easy to reach, to the point of being almost silly. Set the goal to cover a certain length of time. Here are some examples, based on my 100-day walking challenge:

  > Walk 1 mile a day for 100 days

  > Do 15 ab crunches a day for 40 days

  > Eat one piece of fruit every day for 60 days

  > Drink 3 glasses of water every day for 30 days

  > Write 4 sentences in your journal each day for 60 days

  > Spend 10 minutes shooting hoops, kicking a soccer ball, etc., each day for 40 days

  > Spend 10 minutes cleaning out your garage each day for 30 days

  > Get rid of 3 items from your closet each day for 40 days

- Now, get to it. Remember, the larger goal, outside of the literal goal you set for yourself, is to stay the course, to show up every day for yourself, no matter what. You may end up doing more than the minimum requirement some days, and that's great, but on any given day, you only need to do the basic goal.

DAY 3

START SOMEWHERE, ANYWHERE

DURING MY FIRST FIVE YEARS OF LIVING IN the super pricey San Francisco Bay Area, I moved four times. Crazy, right? It wasn't my preference, believe me. But when the market value of my apartment went up $800/month...well, I didn't have much of a choice. The worst part of moving every time was the packing. Like everyone, I hate packing. In the months leading up to each move, I carefully went through all my belongings, getting rid of junk, extra stuff, and things I didn't need or use anymore. My goal was to reduce and eliminate down to only the things I really wanted and needed, to make packing easier.

Without fail, on packing day, I would stand in my apartment and look around, feeling overwhelmed and paralyzed. I didn't know where to begin. Even after my conscious effort to streamline my belongings, I still had a TON of stuff.

Is it best to start in the kitchen, to take the time up front to wrap each plate and pack those awkward pots and pans? Maybe it's better to start with my clothes, because I can easily set aside the few remaining outfits I'll need for the next day or so. No, I should start with my son's room and get all the toys with all their little parts packed and out of the way. Or maybe I should just sit down on my sofa and eat chocolate and cry.

Have you ever felt like that? Overwhelmed with everything that needs done, to the point of not being able to do anything? Maybe you are in school and have so much homework that you just don't know where to start. Should you get the quick and easy math problems out of the way first? Or, is it better to get the heavy essay started, and save the easier stuff for last? Maybe make the outline for the essay, then take a break to play games on your phone, then study for the upcoming quiz, then do the math problems, then hopefully still have time to start the essay? You know what, let's just play games now and then take a nap. Sound familiar?

Maybe it's time to clean your house, and holy cow, when did it get this bad? There's a pile of "important" things covering your dresser, your stove top is splattered, the counter top is covered with drops of who knows what, there are boxes piled by the door that need broken down to get recycled, "stuff" needs to be put away everywhere you look, the bathroom needs cleaned, and holy crap, why is there so much cat hair EVERYWHERE?? (Okay, I admit, that's my current situation).

Maybe there's something you've been wanting to start doing in your life, and the idea's been bouncing around your mind for a while, but so far you haven't done anything about it. Perhaps you'd like to write a book, or learn a new hobby or sport. Maybe you are thinking of going to school, or learning a new skill so you can eventually move on to a different job. Maybe you would like to be in a relationship, or start a family, but haven't taken any action yet because it's really just too overwhelming.

Okay, take a deep breath. In fact, take a nice, big, calming yawn, and stretch really big at the same time. Gently roll your shoulders backwards and frontwards a few times, then shake out your arms and hands. How do you feel? Ready for the next step? Don't worry, the next step is quite easy.

Regardless of what situation you're facing, no matter how overwhelming or complicated or paralyzing it may feel, there's an easy solution.

START SOMEWHERE, ANYWHERE

That sounds almost too easy, and what does it really mean anyway? Shouldn't there be a plan, a strategy, and maybe even a whole crew of people there to help you and guide you and provide moral support along the way? Nope. That's wishful thinking and it's keeping you stuck and frustrated. Just get started. Start somewhere, anywhere.

Most of the time, when you need to get a large and overwhelming project done, it doesn't really matter where you start. Sure, if you brought in someone super analytic, they would probably tell you where to start and how to work your way through your task to be the most efficient and the most coordinated. But, in reality, in most situations it doesn't matter where you start.

Wherever you are, right now, start right there. Literally, right there. I'm sitting at my kitchen counter right now as I write this, and as I look around, I feel a bit overwhelmed with everything that needs done. So, as soon as I put away my laptop, I will start exactly where I am right now, by cleaning the counter. There are some items that need to be put away first, and then I will wipe the countertop. Easy. That will probably, in reality, take me five minutes or less. Then I will do whatever comes next, depending on where I am at that moment. Maybe I'll wipe down the stove top…that will probably take another few minutes, tops. By then, within 5-7 minutes, my kitchen will be looking pretty nice.

There are alternatives to jumping right in. I could just keep sitting at my counter, drinking coffee and trying to ignore the mess, maybe turn on the TV and get lost in an entire series on Netflix. I could make an impressive to-do list that includes about fifty things that need done, with some items even having sub-categories. I'll never get it all done, or by the time it's done it'll be time to start back at the beginning. I could just leave the house and go somewhere. Maybe the cleaning fairies will come and take care of everything while I'm out. (Tried that, doesn't work).. And, after trying these alternatives, I'll feel even more miserable because I still didn't actually get anything done.

A lot of people, including me, tend to feel overwhelmed by seemingly large tasks. There are many reasons why people can struggle with getting things done. I personally can be a bit of a perfectionist, sometimes a little hyper-focused on doing things the right way and getting them done as efficiently as possible. There's usually some self-judgment involved, and then of course there's the guilt that comes if I feel like I'm wasting time.

If you can relate to feeling paralyzed by perfectionism, I want to let you in on something that may be quite freeing to you. Here it is – you don't have to give your 100% effort on every single thing you do. You can give 80% on some tasks and no one, even you, will ever know the difference. Sometimes, when I tell my perfectionist clients this, they straighten their backs, look at me like I'm crazy, and tell me adamantly that they could never do that. I get it. I totally get it. And, please give it a try and see how it goes.

I've learned to be okay with giving my best 80% effort quite often, and what I've found is that my 80% is actually many other people's 100%. No one has ever noticed the difference if I only put 80% of my energy into cleaning my house, or 80% into a project at work. Honestly, I've learned to be okay with giving 60-70% effort to some things, and the world hasn't stopped turning. Experiment with this, and you may soon see your stress level dramatically decrease and your free time increase.

Someone else may feel overwhelmed with starting a large project because they are plagued by their past. They feel like they can't keep their house clean if their childhood home was never clean or was filled with chaos. Or maybe they believe they won't be able to finish something based on their history of starting projects and not finishing them. Maybe they feel like there's no point...the house will be messy again by tomorrow, or there will only be more homework tomorrow and they're still behind from last week. Some people believe they don't deserve a clean house, nice things, or a finished project, based on what they learned during childhood.

If you can relate to those lines of thinking, please remember this: Your thoughts are NOT usually facts and you shouldn't believe most of them. In fact, at least three-quarters of what runs through my head is complete bull and has no basis in reality. (If you need more information on this, refer back to Day 1, Silence the Voices). Grab your companion workbook or journal and write down your thoughts for the next few minutes. Whatever comes to mind, write it down, right now.

Okay, skim your list. How many of those thoughts are actually true? When you start feeling limited by your thoughts, by what you're telling yourself, stop and ask if that thought is a fact, or just some random fluff taking up space in your head. Odds are, if you hear yourself saying, "I can't," or "I don't deserve," or "What's the point," you can immediately shut that down and call BS. Please don't allow fluffy thoughts to stop you from getting started.

If negative feelings get in your way, remind yourself that feelings are not facts, and they also should not stop you from starting something. Yes, your feelings are always valid and you shouldn't ignore how you feel; however, feelings pass by like clouds in the sky, and they are not necessarily even based on facts or reality. Have you ever tried timing one of your feelings? Next time you're feeling sad, irritable, or even elated or excited, look at the clock and see how long it lasts. Two minutes? Maybe ten minutes, tops?

There are a couple quick tricks you can try to change your mood, which you can use anytime, but especially if you feel like a mood is creating a barrier to getting started on something. Next time you're feeling cranky or disgruntled about something, smile. A small, fake smile is sufficient. Literally, curve your lips up, even just halfway, and see how you feel. Still feeling cranky and disgruntled? Probably, but the feelings are likely not nearly as strong. Some researchers suggest doing the small smile briefly, some suggest keeping it for 60 seconds, and some say to hold it for 90 seconds. Regardless, there is agreement that even a superficial half-smile will improve your mood. If you really want to put this to the test, try it the next time someone cuts you off in traffic!

An alternative way to boost your mood is to run the inside of your wrists under cold water, or rub an ice cube behind your ear or across your forehead. Or, end your shower with a burst of cool water. Some people swear by hydrotherapy, and typically cold water is best at treating depression. If the burst of cold water is too shocking, you can gradually cool the water over five minutes, and keep it cool without going too cold. So, ignore your mood, or change your mood, and get started on whatever it is you need to do.

Hopefully we're in agreement that we can all feel overwhelmed by large projects or tasks sometimes, based on personality traits, issues from our past, because of negative thoughts or moods, or simply because a project is huge. That's okay, and you can still start somewhere, anywhere. Let's take a look at some examples of large projects or issues that you may facing right now.

Maybe your overwhelming or complicated project doesn't involve cleaning at all and is something that is supposed to be fun or meant to bring joy and happiness to your future self. Do you want to get in shape, but the thought of planning a workout, creating a food plan, and then trying to fit everything into your schedule stops you in your tracks? Do you want to start your own business, but the details are making you dizzy?

Maybe you have a dream to go to school and complete a degree, but you don't know what you want to focus on, how to apply for financial aid, and if you can even fit school into your already full schedule. Or, maybe you're feeling stuck at your job, but you don't know what to do or where to go. Maybe you're in a new job, and it's not what you thought it was going to be, but the thought of going back to the drawing board is just too much.

Regardless of the task or project you are facing, first of all, please know that many people have already been there, in your shoes, feeling an uncomfortable combination of overwhelming, insecure, and anxious feelings. It's okay. Now, I want you to start somewhere, anywhere, and spend 15-30 minutes doing something, anything, related to the project or task or situation you are facing. Clean out one shelf in the refrigerator and wipe it down. Organize one shelf in your pantry. Open the textbook next to you and start reading. Prepare a healthy snack and have it ready to go in your fridge. Brainstorm a short list of ideas for your business and write them down. Look up the college closest to your home and take note of any courses they offer that interest you. Look through your list of contacts and note the people you could potentially reach out to for advice on changing jobs or careers.

Don't put more than 10 seconds of thought into what you're going to do first. Just do it. Easy. You may want to set your alarm if you are at risk of getting sucked in and overdoing it. Go ahead, right now.

Welcome back. Did you stop after 15-30 minutes? How do you feel? Did you experience any negative outcomes from potentially starting in the "wrong" area? Do you even feel a little motivated and excited, like maybe you could either continue with your current task or move on to another part of your project? If so, go for it! Spend another 15-30 minutes doing something else related to your task. And then stop.

Be sure to take a break every 30-60 minutes, enough time to grab some water or a snack and to stretch. When you have another 15-30 minutes at your disposal, jump right back in, and either pick up where you left off or do something different yet still related to your project. Look at you, you are doing it!

Have you ever heard of "spiraling?" You may have heard about it in the context of someone being on a "downward spiral" where one bad thing led to another in their life. Well, lucky for us, we can also get on an "upward spiral." That's rarely talked about, but it happens all the time, and it's exactly the opposite of a downward spiral. For example, in Day 2, I talked about signing up for the 100-day walking challenge, where I started out by just walking one mile a day. Even though my goal was to just walk, I also started drinking more water, then making some better food decisions, then I added another mile, and then I added running to my walks.

It would have been too much to start out doing everything at once, but I could start with an easy walk, and the momentum from that activity pushed me to make a second healthy choice. The positive energy from doing two healthy things easily led to others. Before I knew it, I was living a fit lifestyle that had overwhelmed me just a few weeks prior.

Upward spirals tend to happen organically, so be patient and trust the process. Take one step, and the next positive step will fall into place naturally. Start somewhere, anywhere, and see where it takes you.

You may have heard the phrase, "one good thing leads to another," and it's the same thing as "upward spiraling." Start small, but start somewhere, anywhere. And then do it again tomorrow. And the next day. You may not be "feeling it," but you are doing it, and your upward spiral is coming. I've seen it happen countless times.

THINKING POINTS:

- Is there a project or task you've been avoiding because it feels too overwhelming or complicated?

- Have you been avoiding starting on something because you feel like you'll never get it done or that you'll burn out in the process?

ACTION ITEMS:

- Don't spend any more time right now thinking about your project, because you've no doubt already thought about it to exhaustion. Be clear on what project, task, or change you are focusing on, and go do something related to it for 15 minutes. It doesn't matter what it is. It may even feel silly or impractical. Set a timer if needed, and get started.

- After 15 minutes, check in with yourself. Did you notice any old thoughts or feelings coming up for you, perhaps related to perfectionism, being overwhelmed, thinking you don't deserve something, or even wondering what's the point in doing such a small part of such a large project? That's okay! Just make note of what came up for you, and carry on.

- Now, spend another 15 minutes working on the same project. You can continue working on the small part you already started, or you can do something else. For example, if you are cleaning your kitchen and you got a pantry shelf cleaned out in the first 15 minutes, then either do another shelf in the second 15 minutes, or clean out a shelf in your fridge or wipe down your counter. Keep breaking it down into these doable, 15-minute increments (or 30 minutes if that's reasonable for you).

- After no more than 30-60 minutes, take a sit-down or stretch break, depending on what you've been doing. Drink some water. You are done for today.

- Congratulate yourself for getting started, and be satisfied with the effort you put in today.

- Do the same thing tomorrow. And then the next day. You only need to spend 15 minutes working on your project on any given day. Anything extra is a bonus, but I caution you to not spend too much time on any particular day, to avoid feeling drained. The point is to start somewhere, anywhere, and you will naturally catch your upward spiral.

DAY 4

JUST BREATHE

I WISH I COULD TELL YOU THAT I meditate every day. That I sit on a meditation cushion for 30 minutes each morning, with my back straight, my gaze down, and my spirit at peace while I breathe slow, deep breaths and just notice my thoughts as they come and go. Meditating has been a goal of mine for as long as I can remember, and although I've tried to meditate many times, it just hasn't really clicked for me yet.

I still subscribe to meditation magazines and read them faithfully, and I can recite to you all the mental and physical benefits of meditating. Unfortunately, when I think of meditating in its purest form, I get anxious. I've even tried lowering my goal to just 5 minutes a day, using a meditation app on my phone, and laying down on the floor because that was more comfortable than sitting on a cushion... still couldn't do it. Within the first 2 minutes I'd find myself rolling over and scrolling through my phone.

Why do I want to learn to meditate so badly? No, not just because it looks cool or because it's trendy. I know that meditation can help to manage stress, bring peace and balance, improve my quality of life as I age, help with my digestion, sleep, and functioning of my internal organs, and just make me a nicer person to be around. Given the amount of internal and external stress we all face, I would argue that we all need the benefits of meditation.

Like everyone, I get stressed out during my workday on a regular basis. My problems don't rise to the level of stressors that many people across the world feel every day, no question about that. But, my stress is very real to me. Even "good stress" that comes from having something new and fun is still stress, and our bodies don't know the difference. And, if I ignore my stress, or minimize it, or say that it's just temporary, or normalize it and say that everyone is stressed so it's okay, I will ultimately pay the price. Do you know what the price is, of living under chronic stress? Depression, anxiety, digestive issues, insomnia, headaches, anger and irritability, chronic pain, cancer, heart disease, systemic diseases, premature death…just to name a few.

As both a psychotherapist and a massage therapist, I can tell you first hand, people are STRESSED OUT. My clients tend to suffer from chronic tension, especially in their neck and shoulders, and they can't sleep well. They are irritable and battle with road rage, they struggle with too many competing priorities in their lives, and when I first meet them and ask them how they're doing, it's always, "busy" or "stressed."

I recently read an article about how people are much more stressed out now compared to in the 1980's, and that the risk of premature death is significantly higher as the result. There's several reasons for the increase in stress, but one clear reason is the rise of technology and the expectation or need to always be connected and accessible. There are other reasons as well, including a turbulent economy, not being able to take vacations, the need to buy more stuff to keep up with everyone else, etc. But speaking from my own experiences, technology and the addictive nature of the internet and social media are the primary culprits for many people.

It is totally possible that my worldview is a bit jaded because I moved to the heart of Silicon Valley nearly ten years ago, where technology is created and competition is intense. People in this region probably tend to be more stressed than elsewhere, and they work longer hours because if they're not producing and advancing technology, someone else will take their place and get ahead. However, I think that if I took a survey around the country and just asked people how they're doing, the most common answers would still be "busy" or "stressed," regardless of where they live.

The good news – you can quickly and easily manage your stress and alleviate that constant "stressed out" feeling reported by so many people. And, it's not hard or complicated or even time consuming! I'm happy to share with you what I've been teaching my clients for many years.

Although I continue to struggle with meditation in its purest form, I've found a few related techniques that release stress, tension and blocked energy, and ease the mind and spirit. In fact, I might even argue that these methods are even more beneficial than pure meditation at managing stress, because they are multidimensional and the results are immediate. They are accessible to me personally because they involve doing more than just sitting, and I prefer doing a couple things at once. The techniques have the same foundation, and to be honest, if you even learn only the foundation, you will see incredible results. The foundation of managing your stress is simple.

JUST BREATHE

Super easy, right? We breathe all the time, and we don't even have to think about it! Well, that is technically correct, however, the way we typically breathe is not very healthy. It's usually shallow and rapid and comes from our chests. Shallow and rapid breathing can cause anxiety or make anxiety worse, and it can even trigger a panic attack. Breathing from the chest also keeps baseline stress level high, which contributes to stress-related diseases and that "stressed out" feeling.

If you're in a room with other people right now, look around at them. Do you see their shoulders moving up and down as they breathe? Can you notice the quick pace and rhythm of their breathing? Poor things, maybe you can go give them some pointers after you finish this chapter.

Okay, back to you. Take a minute and start to notice your own breath. Are you breathing rapidly, from your chest? You probably are, just like everyone else around you, and it's normal. Now, allow your stomach to be soft, and really let it all hang out without worrying about how you look. We're often taught to "suck in our gut" to look slimmer, but when we're breathing properly, we need to do the opposite. Purposely shift your breathing down lower, into your abdomen. This is called "belly breathing."

You can belly breathe while standing, sitting, or lying down. Some people who initially have a hard time breathing from their bellies find it easiest to learn while lying down on their backs. If it's helpful, you can place one hand on your chest and the other hand on your belly. Only your belly hand should be moving while you breathe. (If you'd like to watch a short video on how to belly breathe, please see www. restorebodyandsoul.com/books).

I like to picture a big, red balloon in my stomach, inflating when I inhale, then slowly deflating when I exhale. You should not notice any movement in your shoulders while you are belly breathing, and only your belly should be moving. Go watch yourself breathe in a mirror if you want to confirm that your shoulders are not moving. Your belly should be moving, and you should see it slowly expanding out the front as you inhale, and then returning to normal as you exhale.

Have you ever watched an animal breathe? If you have a cat or dog in your house, watch them while they are sleeping or relaxing.

That's what belly breathing looks like. Have you ever watched a baby breathe? Yup, you guessed it, they breathe from their bellies as well. Belly breathing is how animals (including humans) breathe naturally and instinctively. Unfortunately, stress and social pressure influences humans to start breathing shallowly from their chests, sometimes even from an early age. But don't worry, you can change how you breathe, with practice.

Once you've gotten the hang of belly breathing, keep practicing it. Set an alarm on your phone for several times a day to remind you to stop and check how you're breathing. If you catch yourself breathing from your chest, purposely shift your breathing lower to your belly. Soon it will come more naturally for you.

To enhance the benefits of belly breathing, there are some additional techniques I'd like you to try. I find these techniques easier than meditation (probably because they are a bit more active), and the results are similar if not better, in terms of managing your stress and improving your overall health and wellness. The first involves adding counting to your belly breathing, and the second involves adding acupressure. Let's start with counting your breaths.

First, make sure you are belly breathing. Take several nice, slow, deep belly breaths, close your eyes if you feel comfortable doing do, and settle. Now you are ready to start counting. I will give you the script in a second, but essentially you're going to count as you inhale, then hold your breath at the top, then count as you exhale.

Your exhales should be a bit longer than your inhales, as this helps slow your breathing and increase your relaxation. The short hold at the top is essential to assimilate your oxygen and help your energy flow. Your pace should be approximately one count per second. Before you give it a shot, take a second and notice your current stress level. On a scale of 1-10, with 1 being no stress at all and 10 being totally stressed out, what's your number? Please jot down your number in your companion workbook.

Time to give it a shot. As you inhale, say slowly in your head, "Inhale, 2, 3, 4, hold 2, 3, exhale, 2, 3, 4, 5. Inhale 2, 3, 4, hold 2, 3, exhale, 2, 3, 4, 5." The goal is to extend your breaths longer and longer, so after a few rounds, count to 5 as you inhale and to 6 as you exhale. As you improve, you may even be able to extend to 8 or 9 as you inhale, and 9 or 10 as you exhale. Take your time and enjoy this process. (Please feel free to watch the demonstration at www. restorebodyandsoul.com/books).

There is no rush to increase your counts. The point is to notice your breathing and slow it down. Some people ask if it matters if you breathe from your nose or mouth, and it really doesn't matter. I'm personally more comfortable breathing both in and out my nose, but you can experiment and see what works for you. Just make sure you are still doing your belly breathing.

Time to give it another try. Now that you know the script, do 5-6 rounds of counting your breaths, or even 2-3 minutes. Keep your back straight and comfortable, and close your eyes. Go ahead and put your book down now and settle into it.

How do you feel? Do you notice an immediate difference in the quality of your breathing? Is the level of tension in your stomach, chest, neck and shoulders any less? Re-rate your current stress level on the same scale of 1-10. Has your overall stress level dropped a couple notches? I'm pretty sure you are feeling much better after a very short breathing session.

The second technique to add to your belly breathing is acupressure. You may have never heard of acupressure, but you have likely heard of acupuncture. Acupressure predates acupuncture, and has been used as part of Traditional Chinese Medicine for the past 5,000 years. There is a reason why it's been around that long – it works! Acupressure uses the same "points" as acupuncture, but acupressure uses finger pressure to stimulate the points instead of needles. To put it very simply, acupressure releases energy and tension that is blocked in your body, and when it is released, you feel better physically and mentally, more balanced and healthy.

I first heard of acupressure in massage school. I learned that it was effective in treating headaches, digestive issues, stress, and countless other physical and emotional ailments. After graduating, I continued to study acupressure and eventually went on to complete an Acupressure Mastery Program to really solidify my understanding. I created an Acupressure for Emotional Well-Being class, and I have presented on acupressure to many groups of mental health professionals and mental health clients. I am a big proponent of using acupressure, because it works.

Acupressure is easy to learn and use, plus it's free, you can use it anytime, and it's the perfect complement to Western medicine. I never recommend acupressure in place of Western medicine or medication, but I almost always recommend a holistic wellness plan that includes a healthy diet and exercise, acupressure and deep breathing, and checking in regularly with your primary care doctor.

My clients who attend my class, and who have incorporated acupressure into their daily routines, have seen some pretty incredible results. They report that they sleep well now, when they used to have insomnia. Some report being able to take less medication for depression and anxiety. They have better interactions with their family members, when they used to be irritable and angry. Some have seen a lessening in their grief. They can breathe better, have improved posture and less physical pain. They experience less cravings for sugar, tobacco and other harmful substances, and report feeling lighter and happier. One person even lost a significant amount of weight after making some of the healthy dietary changes recommended in class (e.g., reducing fatty and fried foods and soda, all which mess up your energy flow).

Explaining in detail how acupressure works, how to hold a point, and what points to use to address specific issues is beyond the scope of this book. However, I invite you to view a free video on my website (www.restorebodyandsoul.com/acupressure) to learn more about how acupressure works, and to learn some common, powerful points. And, if you are interested, you can download whole classes or schedule an individual session with me that addresses specific physical and emotional imbalances.

Although I struggle with sitting in pure meditation, holding an acupressure point for 2-3 minutes while breathing deeply is very accessible for me, and extremely beneficial. Literally, a couple minutes here and there, along with your belly breathing, is all you need to drastically reduce that "stressed out" feeling and lower the risk of developing stress-related health and emotional problems. If you already have some ailments, it's likely you will notice a decrease in your symptoms. Just let your doctor know you are doing acupressure regularly, because your medications may need to be adjusted and possibly decreased.

So, how are you feeling about belly breathing, counting your breaths, and giving acupressure a try? We've covered quite a bit in this chapter, but I can't emphasize enough how important breathing is in managing your stress and improving your overall health. I included extra space in your companion workbook, just behind the Action Items for this chapter, where you can track your progress (on the 1-10 stress scale) and see if these techniques are working for you.

Your breathing and acupressure sessions can literally be anywhere from a minute or two to as long as 20-30 minutes. And, there's no need to watch the clock, because it really doesn't matter how long you count your breaths or hold a point...you will know when you start feeling better.

THINKING POINTS:

- How do you typically breathe? From your chest or from your belly?

- When you consciously shift your breathing lower, what immediate physical and emotional changes do you notice?

- Do you currently have any potentially stress-related physical or emotional ailments that could be reduced by regularly using belly breathing, counting breaths, or acupressure?

ACTION ITEMS:

- Practice belly breathing right now, then again when you're lying in bed tonight, and again when you wake up in the morning. Repeat throughout your day, and set an alarm if needed to remind you to check in on how you're breathing.

- Set aside time to count your breaths. You might start at just 30 seconds, or 4-5 rounds of breathing. Count to 4 as you inhale, then hold your breath for 2 counts, then exhale for 5 counts. Gradually work towards increasing your time and increasing your numbers, but there is no rush. You will likely see immediate benefits after counting your breaths for just 30 seconds. (You can practice with me on my website at www.restorebodyandsoul.com/books).

- Watch the free video on how acupressure works and learn a few key points on my website (www.restorebodyandsoul.com/acupressure).

- Track your progress in your workbook or journal. Note how your stress level can drop after even a very short session.

DAY 5

SHOW YOURSELF COMPASSION

I PUT A LOT OF PRESSURE ON MYSELF. I always have. I'm not competitive when it comes to athletics or sports teams, and you probably don't want me on your team for board games because winning just isn't important to me. But, I am fiercely competitive with myself. I don't need to be perfect, but I was born with a very strong internal motivation that drives me to always do more and reach the highest level of whatever it is I'm trying to achieve. I'm sure there are some people who admire my drive and stamina and perseverance. I like to look at my strong personal motivation as a good thing...until I don't reach a goal or measure up to the standards I set for myself. Then it's not such a good characteristic to have.

Certain things tend to come easy for me. Growing up, getting good grades came naturally for me. I graduated near the top of my high school class, from college with Magna Cum Laude status...you get my point. Interestingly, even though school was easy for me, I never felt very smart inside. Sometimes I even felt like a fraud. I could memorize facts and manipulate numbers (which led to getting A's), but I struggled with retaining information past the tests and with applying the information more broadly. I worried what would happen if someone found out. Heaven forbid, what if a teacher put me on the spot and asked me to take a concept we learned and apply it to a different context?

Well, someone did find out. And the embarrassment, no, the humiliation, was worse than I had ever imagined.

When my son turned three, I decided to go back to school to get my PhD in social work. One of my undergraduate professors had planted the PhD-seed in me many years ago, and that had never left me. I was going through a difficult time at that point in my life and was needing something positive to focus on, so I applied to an elite doctoral program and was accepted. Only three people started the program at the same time as me, and I could immediately tell that this program was going to challenge me in ways I'd never been challenged before.

I took three courses my first semester, and they were all very difficult for me. In my statistics class, we had to learn not only how to do statistics, but also how to code in a very old and unforgiving computer program. I had taken statistics as an undergrad, but this course was nothing like I'd previously experienced. However, although I struggled a lot, I (barely) survived and passed the exams.

The other two classes were nearly impossible for me. They were classes that involved reading large, heavy, incomprehensible books, and then participating in classroom discussions. The discussions started out by mentioning the book, but then they always grew into abstract debates of concepts that I can't even begin to explain to you. This was my worst nightmare, worse than the dream of showing up to class in your underwear. I couldn't keep up. I felt so simple-minded compared to everyone else in the class. I tried to plan ahead by writing comments in my books, that I could potentially make in class if the discussion went a certain way, but that never really worked out. In class, I tried to fake it by keeping a knowing look on my face while I sat quietly and everyone else talked, but I don't think I fooled anyone.

On the hour and a half drive home each day, I alternated between crying and mentally beating myself up for how stupid I was. See? I really wasn't smart. I knew it all along. I should've never tried getting my PhD. What if I couldn't finish this program and had to drop out because I couldn't keep up? What would people think? Everyone always thought I was so smart, and now that wasn't true any longer. What would my son think someday? I put myself down so much during those long commutes that it was hard to pick myself up and carry on when I finally got home.

One day I got back a paper I had written, and on the bottom my professor asked to see me. Although she was technically a social worker, and social workers tend to be quite nice, she was not a kind person, not in class and not when we were alone. She scared me, and I was trembling when I went to meet with her.

She had me sit down, and then she asked me what I was doing in the program. I don't remember my response, because my response didn't matter anyway. She went on to tell me that my paper didn't meet the standards of the program. She said that the students in that program were naturally very intelligent, even brilliant. They were able to think abstractly and draw connections between concepts that created new ideas and meanings. She said that I worked very hard, and that I had gotten good grades throughout my life simply because I was a hard worker. She said I could only think concretely, and abstract thoughts were beyond me. She said I didn't fit in with the other students in the program. I wasn't naturally smart enough and working hard wasn't going to save me this time.

She was so smug. She had no problem telling me these things, as I sat there quietly. I didn't argue with her. I felt shocked, hurt, embarrassed, ashamed and sad. Was she right? She was only echoing what I had been telling myself my whole life, but I didn't ever think someone would just come right out and say those things to me.

I met with the program director soon after that. He was nicer towards me, and he had kind eyes and a softer demeanor. He told me, "You can't know what you don't know," and he was right. I came to the conclusion that I wasn't going to make it through that program. I wasn't naturally brilliant, which was apparently a pre-requisite for that school, and all the hard work in the world wasn't going to help me succeed there. The negative self-talk really took over at that point. I won't even repeat some of the mean things I said to myself.

Once my negative self-talk took a breather, I started taking an inventory of myself. This did not happen overnight, believe me, but I did eventually get to the point where I could start seeing my strengths again. I may not be a genius, but I had nailed high school, college and grad school. I really was a hard worker, and I was incredibly organized and motivated and paid careful attention to detail. That had to count for something. I had a strong sense of empathy for people in need, and I wanted to get my doctoral degree so I could teach and do research and help people on a broader level. I wanted to reach the highest degree in my field and set a good example for my son. Above all, I was a kind-hearted, loving person, which I think is more important than anything.

I started wondering if it really mattered whether I had ever "felt smart." If I could do well in school and at work and still maintain a sense of morality, then…maybe I didn't actually have a problem. Although I initially thought my professor discovered my "secret," could it be that maybe the program wasn't so great after all? Perhaps there was a reason that only two other people started the program with me, instead of a regular-sized class.

It was hard to bounce back, I'm not going to lie. That professor really laid my worst insecurities bare and called out my vulnerabilities like she was ordering coffee. But you know what? I did bounce back. I applied to another doctoral program, and I got in and made my way. I still didn't participate much in class discussions. I still felt like I couldn't always keep up with the sharpest minds in the class, but I made it.

The professors in my new program were all incredibly kind, warm, and supportive. They wanted all of the students to succeed, and they knew that our success was a reflection of them. I rocked statistics in my new program and was asked to be the teacher's assistant for the next group of students. My research professor asked to use one of my papers as an example for future classes.

I could work hard and earn my PhD in a highly rated social work program, even if I wasn't naturally brilliant.

I learned a lot through that whole experience. The most important thing – you can bounce back after you've been knocked down. You can carry onward and upward even after a lifetime of being beaten down by yourself or others. It's easy to say, but not easy to do.

SHOW YOURSELF COMPASSION

Maybe you had a time in your life where you had a setback and all you could hear was that negative voice in your head (or other people's voices telling you negative things). Perhaps your entire life was a series of knock-downs, and that negative voice is the only voice you've ever heard. I'm here to let you know that you can recover from that. No matter what you've been through, what you've seen, what you've experienced, there is a way to turn things around. Show yourself compassion.

What does that mean, to show yourself compassion? It means giving yourself a break, and talking to yourself the way you'd talk to a friend. When I was telling you about how that professor told me I wasn't smart enough to fit in with the rest of the students, did you feel sad for me? Did you want to tell me that it was going to be okay, that I was a good person, that I was smart, and that she was the one with the problem? Those are some examples of compassionate statements.

It can feel awkward and uncomfortable to talk to yourself in a compassionate manner, especially if you've never done it before. Right now, take a minute and think about yourself, and acknowledge how you're taking this time to work on yourself, and give yourself credit for working hard and trying your best. You may not believe what you're saying to yourself, and that's okay. You may feel silly and inauthentic – no worries at all! Stick with it, keep using kind words when you talk to yourself, and eventually you will believe them. Keep saying it in your head, and soon your heart will follow.

If you find this really challenging, try splitting yourself up, and talk to the different parts of you. Stay with me here; this is not as crazy as it sounds. We all have many parts of ourselves…the child, the rebellious teenager, the responsible adult, the carefree spirit, etc… right? Try making a compassionate statement only to the child-part of yourself. Acknowledge the difficulties the rebellious teenager-part is having. Congratulate the responsible adult-part for taking care of business. Show some love for the carefree-part. Is that a bit easier? Just keep practicing. Being able to show yourself compassion is a skill that will come in handy throughout your life.

Another way to show yourself compassion is by listening to your cues, or your internal warning system. This is something I've been working on for a while now, and I'll explain what I mean. When we get busy, or stressed out, or caught up with believing the negative voices in our heads, usually the first thing we stop doing is listening to our own cues. Our bodies let us know when we're hungry, tired, thirsty, overwhelmed, sick, sad, stressed, exhausted, etc., and we quickly learn to ignore those important messages.

Unfortunately, in today's world, we do our best to disregard these cues because we need to work harder and faster, be more productive, be stronger and never show weakness, keep going because there's always someone to take your place. Ultimately, we pay the price when we don't listen to our cues, and we end up physically sick and emotionally imbalanced.

When was the last time you listened to your cues? Can you even remember? I've really only started paying attention to my cues in the past few years, but now checking in with myself is part of my daily routine. How do I check in with myself? I make myself the main priority in my life, and making sure my own needs are met is something I do every day. "But that's so selfish!" "My family comes first!" "My job is my priority!" I used to hear the same thoughts in my head, until I realized that no one benefits when I am hungry, tired, stressed, or any of those other things I mentioned. Show yourself compassion.

So now I check in with myself throughout the day, every day, to see how I'm doing. If I'm hungry, I get a snack. If I'm tired, I take a 10-minute nap. If I'm stressed, I breathe deeply, and make a reasonable plan for what needs done. And then each and every evening, I go for a walk outside, take time to relax, and several times a week I soak in an amazing, restorative milk bath. (Check out my website if you want the recipe, www.restorebodyandsoul.com/books).

Can you try listening to your cues right now? Really tune in to your body and see if it's trying to tell you anything. Are you thirsty? Are your shoulders riding up from stress? Do you need to stretch? When was the last time you ate? Are you breathing slowly and deeply, or rapidly and shallowly? Is there anything you need right now?

Show yourself compassion by listening to your cues and establishing a daily ritual that addresses your needs. There's no denying the mind-body connection, and showing yourself compassion in both the way you talk to yourself and in how you treat your body and your body's needs are equally important. Please, make this a priority, so you can truly be the best you.

THINKING POINTS:

- When was the last time you showed yourself compassion in the way you talk to yourself? Do you remember?

- Do you find it easier to treat others or yourself with compassion?

- Is this a new concept to you, or is this something you're already skilled at? If this is brand new for you, I encourage you to spend some extra time on this chapter.

- How do you typically talk to yourself? Do you treat yourself like you would a friend, or do you say things you would never actually say out loud to anyone else?

- Do you listen to the cues your body gives you (e.g., hungry, thirsty, tired, stressed, sick, etc.), or have you learned to ignore them? Are you meeting your own needs each day and throughout the day? If not, why not?

- Start thinking about what you want in your daily ritual that will meet your needs and also feel amazing. For example, if you tend to feel stressed, your daily ritual may include hot herbal tea, a lavender bath, and time with a good book. If you tend to feel cranky and low energy, your daily routine may involve creating and eating five healthy snacks that ease your irritability and bring you more energy. If you sit at work all day with your shoulders up to your ears and your back hunched over, your ritual may involve some nice yoga stretches, massaging your own neck or getting regular professional massages, and taking a walk.

ACTION ITEMS:

- Select a four-hour timeframe either today or tomorrow, and really pay attention to what you're telling yourself as you go about your regular routine. Grab a sticky note, make a line down the middle, and draw a plus sign at the top of one side and a minus sign at the top of the other side. (Or use the space I created for you in the companion workbook). Make a slash on the plus side each time you tell yourself something kind or compassionate, and make a slash on the minus side each time you tell yourself something unkind or negative. At the end of the four hours, count how many positive and negative slashes you have. Are you surprised? Is this an area that needs more attention?

- Start tuning into your cues today. If you're not used to listening to your cues, set an alarm for the top of each hour, and ask yourself the following questions each time it goes off. Am I hungry? Am I thirsty? Am I tired, stressed, overwhelmed, sick, tense, or in need of a break? Personalize your list of questions, and then show yourself compassion by taking care of that need.

- Establish a daily ritual, starting today or tomorrow, that incorporates meeting the needs you have each day while also feeling like the highlight of your day. This routine doesn't need to take much time, and even 10-20 minutes is a great start. Do you already have everything you need? Your daily ritual doesn't need to be expensive or cost any money at all. Just be sure you have everything in place that you need, and protect your time so that nothing will deter you.

DAY 6

LET IT GO

MANY YEARS AGO, I WAS ATTENDING A CHURCH service in Lancaster County, PA. It was at a church that wasn't overly "religious" and instead focused more on life lessons. The pastor told a story I never forgot. He told the story of a child who was playing a long and complicated game of Monopoly with his family. The child worked very hard, buying and selling his properties, growing his fortune, and celebrating the victories that kept coming to him as he grew richer and owned more properties.

After several hours, it was time to end the game, and the child was disappointed and upset. He had worked so hard to accumulate all his stuff and he didn't want to put everything away. His grandmother, who had been playing the game with him, gently explained that the game was over, and it all must go back in the box. It was fun while it lasted, collecting things that felt valuable and important, and thus the boy felt valuable and important. But, when it was over, it all went back in the box.

Can you relate to that boy? Believing that value and importance comes from how much we accumulate? I know I can. For most of my life, I thought "success" was defined by what or how much I owned. Being a social worker, I've never had enough money to purchase large homes or expensive cars, however, I still accrued a lot of…stuff.

I collected more and more, thinking it was making me happier and happier. Having cabinets packed full of every kitchen appliance and tool imaginable, closets and drawers bursting with clothing that I'd never wear (or wear again), "junk" drawers that could barely close filled with who knows what. Sound familiar? I may not be able to afford a lot of luxuries in life, but I sure owned a ton of crap. And for what purpose? The message from that church service from all those years ago never left me. I can't take anything with me when my time on earth is complete. When this game is over, it all goes back in the box. So why was my house still jam-packed with stuff?

Several months ago, I heard about a documentary called "Minimalism" on Netflix. I watched it, and then immediately bought and read the book it was based on. The documentary and book follow the lives of Joshua Fields Millburn and Ryan Nicodemus, known as "The Minimalists," and their journeys to minimalism. Their message, while simple, changed my life dramatically.

After watching that documentary, I did some soul searching, and I realized that even though I knew my belongings weren't going to last forever or travel with me into eternity, I was subconsciously trying to fill a void in my life by holding on to them. We're taught very young that it's important to earn money to buy stuff, that stuff is important, and that if you don't have stuff, you're not important. It's never spelled out that clearly, but that message is part of every advertisement we see on television, in magazines, and on social media, every day of our lives from the time we are little children.

If I didn't have all my stuff, who was I? If I didn't own an outfit for every day of the year (only a slight exaggeration), I'm not worthy. I can't get rid of my extra wooden spoons, even if I have twenty of them...that would be wasteful and wrong. I shouldn't throw out all those random buttons and paper clips and pens and nearly empty lotion bottles...I may need them someday and then regret trashing them. Nope, can't ever throw out old socks and underwear even though they're clearly unwearable, because what will happen if I ever run out of clean socks and underwear?

When I really got inside my head, I was pretty surprised at my automatic thoughts, about why I was holding onto so much stuff. Yes, part of the reason was because I was materialistic, and I worried that if I didn't have "enough" of something (meaning, an abundance of something), then I was "less than."

But on top of pure materialism, there were other reasons why I was holding onto everything. To summarize, I was living in a house packed with all kinds of stuff because 1) I'm worthless without it; 2) I don't want to feel wasteful; and 3) I fear being caught unprepared. Digging deep, I don't actually believe those things, and yet I was living my life with those notions subconsciously driving me.

Once I got to the heart of the matter, and realized why I was holding onto everything, I was able to consciously rationalize that 1) I'm personally valuable, no matter what I own; 2) I can get rid of things without feeling wasteful; and 3) Holding on to random things doesn't actually make me more prepared for anything. In other words, the automatic thoughts I'd been telling myself were not valid, and I'd carted my stuff through six different moves, including one across the country, for no good reason.

Now back to the documentary that prompted me to take a closer look at my house, life, beliefs, and values. Minimalism. What does that mean?

The idea of minimalism isn't to simply get rid of all your stuff and sit alone in an empty house that looks uninhabited. Not at all! It's about purposely and thoughtfully removing everything from your life that you don't absolutely need, and anything that doesn't hold great value to you, in order to make room for what is really important. It's not about decluttering or getting organized; it's about being intentional.

If you don't absolutely treasure or love an item, or use the item almost daily, or sincerely need the item for any real purpose, then get rid of it. Sell it, donate it, set it out on the curb with a "free" sign, throw it away, get rid of it. What's left, after minimizing? Items that you treasure, valuable time that you used to spend on cleaning and organizing, mental space that you didn't even realize was being filled with stress from bursting closets and cabinets, physical room for family, friends, pets, and more personal time. The important things in life.

The message that these guys were spreading really spoke to me. I had been subconsciously conflicted and therefore felt unexplained stress for so long, holding onto so much stuff thinking that it was necessary even while knowing that nothing in this life is truly permanent. Minimalism changed my life.

The more I learned about minimalism, and the more I eliminated from my house, the better I felt. Who knew that owning more and more stuff actually adds stress to your life? I thought the purpose of life was to earn more money to buy more stuff. I was so wrong. Think about it. When you open a drawer in your kitchen to put away a pair of tongs, and you have to wrestle everything around just to squeeze it in so the drawer can close, how do you feel?

When you go to your closet, find shirts that are "hanging" there even without a hanger because it's so packed, and yet you have nothing to wear, how do you feel? When you need some tape, and you have to empty the entire junk drawer to find it, how do you feel? When you open your garage door, or your shed door, or think about your storage unit...well, let's not even go there. Let me sum it up for you: Stuff=Stress.

LET IT GO

Right now, if you're at home, get up and walk around your space. Pretend that you're in someone else's house, and this is the first time you're visiting. What do you see? Look in the closets, open the drawers, look under the bathroom sinks, peek in the basement or garage. Right now, put down this book and go take a couple minutes to look around. Don't worry, I will be right here waiting for you.

Did you find any empty drawers or cabinets? Any empty space on the kitchen counters or under the sinks? What did you feel as you walked around? Did any picture or piece of artwork catch your eye? Did you notice anything that was truly special or beautiful?

I'm not sure what your reaction was to that exercise, but mine was pretty dramatic. I was shocked, really flabbergasted at all the "junk" in my house. I didn't have a messy house, but every drawer and cabinet and closet was jam-packed full of stuff. After that walk-through, I felt a sense of urgency, like I had to start removing things right away. The disconnect between feeling like I needed to own a ton of stuff and feeling stressed out by all the stuff I owned finally made sense to me. I understood my need to accumulate, like the boy playing the Monopoly game, and I understood that the stuff I was accumulating wasn't what was truly valuable to me.

So I got started. The Minimalists have some great suggestions on how to minimize, so please check out their books and blogs for ideas or guidance. For example, they have a great 30-day challenge that might help motivate you and structure your process. Me, I just jumped right in and started on my closet. (For more info on jumping right in, please refer to Day 3, Start Somewhere, Anywhere). I began with my shirts. Every shirt that I hadn't worn in the past year went on a pile on my bed. Turns out I had a lot of shirts that I'd been holding onto for when I lose weight, that shrank or stretched just enough that I couldn't comfortably wear them, and that I've had for so many years that I just don't wear them any longer. Let it go.

As I moved through my pants, jeans, sweatshirts, scarves and belts, the pile on my bed became a mountain. And, with each item I removed from my closet, I felt like I could breathe easier. As my closet emptied of the items I didn't wear or love, I felt lighter and happier. When I finished, I walked in my closet, and saw only the items I loved and the clothes that fit me perfectly today. They hung on hangers, with room to spare on either side of each item. I was overcome with a feeling of freedom, of peace. I knew in my head that clearing out my closet would give me more space and less stress, but the overwhelming feeling of joy was unexpected. I kept walking back into my closet, and automatically taking a deep breath when I entered. It was a powerful experience, and I hope you give it try.

If you were to walk into my house right now, peek in my kitchen cabinets and pantry, open my closet and drawers, you probably wouldn't immediately say, 'wow, a minimalist lives here!'. But, you would notice that the kitchen counters only hold the appliances that are used daily, and that most of the countertops are clear. You would notice that there is space in my closet, and my clothes hanging freely. You would see the socks and underwear that I actually wear, not all of the undergarments that I purchased over the past 15+ years (which was what I found when I first started minimizing). You would look at the walls in my house now and only see the pictures that are incredibly meaningful to my family, and nothing additional to fill the space. You will not find a junk drawer in my house, although you may now find an empty drawer or cabinet.

Even more important than the space on my counters and in my closet, is the time that was created in my life. I don't spend much time cleaning, and to be completely honest, we can easily get away with cleaning our house once or twice a month with some quick touch-ups here and there. I now have time to do more fun activities with my family, without feeling like I need to get home to clean and organize. I have time to exercise, write, pursue my hobbies, and soak in the bathtub for hours at a time. Before minimizing, I carried a burden that I didn't even know was there, and the difference is pretty incredible.

Let it go. Make room in your life for what matters. You can't take anything with you when you leave this earth, not even the clothes on your back. Don't waste your money accumulating things that aren't valuable or meaningful to you. Doing so will only add stress, anxiety, frustration and unhappiness to your life. First, start minimizing, eliminating, clearing out. Next, fill your space and time with what is meaningful and valuable to you. This is how you create the best YOU.

THINKING POINTS:

- What is your house like? If you were visiting for the first time, what would you notice? How would you feel as you walked through each room and peeked in the closets, drawers, and cabinets? Would you feel differently in different parts of the house? Are certain places packed full of stuff? Do you notice any empty space anywhere?

- If you realize that you have a lot of belongings, that every drawer and closet is packed full of stuff, spend some time trying to figure out why. Is having a lot of stuff a status symbol for you? Are you afraid to be caught in a situation where you need something and don't have it? Do you take comfort being surrounded by your stuff? Why are you holding on to things you don't need (or even like)?

- Start thinking about what you might like to do with the extra time and space you will have. What is important, valuable, meaningful, special to you?

- Acknowledge all that you have and how hard you worked to accumulate everything you have. Be thankful, and now prepare to let it go.

ACTION ITEMS:

- Start small. Choose one cabinet or drawer, or set the timer so you spend only 10 minutes in your closet, and start letting things go. Make piles to sell, donate and throw away. One recommendation – don't get caught up in selling every little thing. For the time and effort it takes to make a dollar at a yard sale, it's not worth it, unless you have a ton of dollar items and a free day on your hands. Consider donating your gently-used belongings to Goodwill or posting them for free on a neighborhood app like NextDoor, and you'll find the happiness and ease in doing so outweighs the value of the dollars you would've earned at a yard sale.

- Check out the Minimalist's website at www.theminimalists. com. They have a series of essays and podcasts available for free, and I highly recommend also watching their documentary and reading their book.

- Once you've eliminated the meaningless stuff from your living space, decide what you want in your house, and how you want to spend the time that has opened as the result of having less stuff. Everyone has different views of what they find meaningful and valuable, and I encourage you to take your time. You may feel a bit uncomfortable initially with your extra space and time, but really be thoughtful and don't rush to refill your house or your schedule. Letting go is truly a gift to yourself, so enjoy the process.

FIND BALANCE

I COME FROM A FAMILY DEDICATED TO EATING marshmallows almost every day. I know, that probably sounds silly, but it's true. I think it's genetic. When I was growing up, my mom, sister and I always ate marshmallows. I remember being little and watching my mom eat marshmallows straight from the bag when she got home from work and was starting to prepare dinner. My sister and I loved to put marshmallows, peanut butter and chocolate chips in a bowl and melt it all together in the microwave for about 20 seconds...then stir it into a gooey, stringy mess and eat it warm. Makes my mouth water just thinking about it.

As I've gotten older, my marshmallow preferences have changed slightly. I've actually turned into my mom, and I usually eat them straight from the bag after work during dinner preparation, or even before bed. But the fact remains that I eat marshmallows almost every day. If I miss a day, it's not because I wanted to, but probably because I didn't get to replenish my supply or I was away and forgot to pack them. (Yes, I will pack marshmallows when I travel).

To clarify, I don't eat an entire bag of marshmallows each day. I'm aware of what marshmallows are made of (poisonous sugar) and the damaging effects that sugar has on our bodies and minds. On average, I eat 2-4 marshmallows a day. I'm perfectly content with that amount and I don't need to use willpower to stop at just a few bites.

Now, there are days when I want something more, and on those days, I'll make s'mores with crackers (any kind will do), peanut butter (extra protein and flavor), chocolate chips, and marshmallows, melted in the microwave for about 15 seconds each. It's very rare, but I do admit to already having s'mores as my entire dinner, along with a tall glass of cold milk.

So why am I going on and on about my love for marshmallows, and my desire to eat marshmallows every day? Because eating marshmallows makes me happy. Really, really happy. There are many things in life that I enjoy and love, but honestly, if someone asked me what makes me happy, marshmallows just might be the first thing I say. Can you relate? Is there something in your life that makes you unexplainably happy? Don't attach any judgment, just think about whether there is something that, no matter how crabby or cranky you feel, the mention of that one thing raises your eyebrows and perks you right up.

There have been many times over the course of my life when I tried very hard to change something about myself, with the goal of becoming healthier, fitter, slimmer, stronger. For example, I've committed to some rather extreme diet and exercise plans, and some less extreme but still 100% healthy diet and fitness routines. I usually stuck with some of them for a week or two, or even a month or two if I was really "good," but do you know what I learned?

Eating marshmallows wasn't part of any of those super healthy diet and exercise plans. I know, I couldn't believe it either! Not one of them! Every time I made my health my top priority, out went the marshmallows. (To clarify, I never actually threw away any marshmallows, I just ate them all before I started the plan). Marshmallows have zero nutritional value, are made of sugar and preservatives, turn to fat after eating them, throw off your natural energy balance, screw with your blood sugar, and they are definitely not part of any semi-healthy diet plan out there. Marshmallows are "bad," I get it.

So, every time I set out to make a change or start a new, healthy habit in my life, I eliminated marshmallows. And you know what happened? I was unhappy, and after a short period of time, I failed. And when I failed, I not only went back to my starting point, I usually went to a point that was worse than when I started (gained more weight, stopped exercising completely, etc.). Have you ever had that happen? Not only did you not reach your goal, but you ended up worse off than when you started? Talk about frustrating!

Our brains and bodies resist change so hard – the status quo is what we instinctively want because it's easy and doesn't require effort. But, the typical American status quo, at least when it comes to diet and exercise, isn't ideal, even though we all know we will feel better if we eat a healthier diet and have a regular exercise routine.

I think a big part of the reason why I didn't reach the goals I set out to accomplish was related to one very important thing – I was unhappy! We rarely experience moments of true happiness in our stressful, hectic lives, and now I had purposely eliminated the few moments of true bliss I could count on each day.

Now, I would guess that most of you don't like marshmallows and you could easily live your lives without ever eating a marshmallow. (That does break my heart a little, I must say). So, what is your "marshmallow"? What makes you happy no matter what? What gives you a little boost to get through the day? Is there something you can do each day or a few days a week, a "guilty pleasure," that won't deter you from your goals, and that could actually increase the likelihood of reaching your larger goal?

Maybe you have a goal that is not related to health or fitness, and you can relate to jumping in with both feet. Perhaps you want to learn a new skill, and you devoted all your free time to learning it, only to burn out after a week or two. Maybe you want to be in a relationship, and you spent every spare moment trying to enhance your looks or personality or lifestyle, to the point where you ended up missing out on the fun things you normally enjoy. Or, perhaps you want to be the ideal parent, so you spent every minute reading parenting books, creating learning experiences for your child, and taking educational field trips, only to find that you no longer had time or energy for the things that make you feel happy and whole. Maybe you want to learn meditation so you set your alarm for 4am every day with a plan to get up and sit in silence for an hour, only to hit snooze on the second day.

Can you relate to this "all or nothing" way of thinking, that is common for so many of us when we try to reach a goal? Do you feel like you must give 100% of yourself when you set a goal, and if you don't, well, you may as well throw in the towel? How has that been working for you?

FIND BALANCE

What if you tweaked your goal plan just a little, enough to add a "treat" into your daily or weekly schedule? Maybe you enjoy a small piece of chocolate each morning with your coffee, or you watch one episode of your favorite show once or twice a week, or you have a weekly lunch date or phone call with a friend. What is something that makes you happy, that you really enjoy, and including it in your life could actually improve the odds of you reaching your larger goals? This "thing" wouldn't derail you from reaching your goals, or distract you from what's important, but it would make you happy and give you just enough of a boost to keep going.

When I was in my twenties and early thirties, I really tried to give my all to everything I set out to do. If I didn't give 100%, well, that was the same as failing. And, I often did fail, because putting forth 100% effort for the long-term was too extreme and not sustainable for me. Humans are wired to seek pleasure, and I don't know about you, but I like to be happy sometimes and not dwell on what I can't have. I ended up feeling frustrated, guilty, and defeated after each failure.

I kind of went to the opposite extreme in my later thirties. I think I subconsciously got tired of trying so hard all the time, and my internal pendulum swung the opposite way. Instead of buying healthy recipe books and keeping my cabinets stocked with healthy options, I ate out a LOT. There were weeks, a lot of weeks, when I would eat out up to five or six times. And exercise was a rare occasion, followed by a couple days of sore muscles, then several more weeks of inactivity. And I paid the price.

I thought I could justify it. I was very busy with trying to balance work, school and taking care of things at home. I don't enjoy cooking. And, most of all, I like to eat out with my family because it gives us the chance to all sit down together and enjoy our time without having to worry about grocery shopping, preparing food, or cleaning up. And, I would order whatever I wanted and eat the whole thing, because it was fun and I didn't want to miss out on any part of the experience.

Consequently, I gained fifteen pounds, spent an enormous amount of money at restaurants, and I taught my son that it's okay to eat out all the time. I ignored the scale, assumed I was gaining weight because I was getting older and that's just what happens, and I thought I deserved to be happy at dinner, after working so hard all day and knowing that I had more work to do after dinner.

I went for my annual physical, and my doctor, who is so sweet and kind, kept mentioning my weight gain throughout the visit, saying in a skeptical tone, "well, you're not overweight....". She never finished that sentence, but I got her point and I heard the implied "yet." I had gained weight, and in fact I was heavier than I had ever been excluding when I was pregnant. I was on an unhealthy path at a time in my life where I needed to be creating and solidifying healthy diet and exercise patterns that would set me up for a healthy second half of my life.

That was a wake-up call for me. My extreme thinking, whether it was "too much" or "too little," needed to stop. I made some immediate changes. For example, I added daily exercise back into my schedule, but this time, it was sustainable. My initial goal was to do ten modified push-ups a day. That was it, just do a few easy push-ups (that actually weren't that easy when I first started). Then I added a short evening walk to my days. I didn't track the length or try to keep a certain speed, I just went for a walk around the neighborhood. I gradually and naturally increased my workouts but I never reverted to setting extreme goals for myself. I just told myself to "do something every day, it doesn't matter what it is." Find balance.

My family started eating at home most days of the week. I didn't develop a love of cooking, and I don't think I ever will, but I put together some quick and easy meals. We sat down together to eat, at the table, which was something we had never done at home. When we did eat out, I took along my own take-out container, and before I began eating, I put half of my meal in the container to save for the next day. (There's always at least two servings in every restaurant meal).

I turned forty last year, and I'm at a pretty good place in my life right now. I've found balance in most areas, and I know what works for me to stay healthy and fit for the long-term. I'm no longer obsessed with having the perfect diet, the perfect exercise program, or the perfect body. I exercise every day, but some days that just means going for a short walk. I'm in the process of losing the weight I had put on, and there's no rush. I don't feel the urgency that used to plague me; now I'm making good choices so I can stay healthy for the rest of my life.

I track what I eat every day – not to the extreme of weighing and measuring my food, but just noting briefly what I ate, and also what I weighed that morning, and what exercise I did that day. Doing that helps me stay focused without going overboard. And can you guess what shows up in my food tracker each day? MARSHMALLOWS. Knowing that I can have marshmallows every day makes me happy, it gives me a boost like nothing else can, and it takes away those feelings of deprivation that ultimately lead to failure. And, I'm still reaching my goals and feeling great.

Would I reach my goals faster if I eliminated this extra sugar from my life? Maybe initially, because I would have less carbs and sugar each day. But if the past predicts the future, I would eventually fail because I know myself, and I do a better overall job of staying on track and balanced when marshmallows are in my life. I don't feel guilty when I eat marshmallows, and I don't have to "sneak" them or rationalize why I need to have them or not. I just eat them and am in heaven.

THINKING POINTS:

- Do you tend to have "all or nothing" thinking in one (or many) parts of your life? Is so, what are some examples of where you're unbalanced? How has that been working for you?

- Have you ever set a goal, committed to giving it your 100%, and then felt defeated when you failed after a few days or weeks?

- Are you willing to have slightly slower progress towards your goal, knowing that you will ultimately reach it and maybe have a little more fun along the way?

ACTION ITEMS:

- Think of several things that make you happy. Guilty pleasures, so to speak. This list can include things you've eliminated in the name of reaching your goal, or things you would like to do or have. What makes you really, really happy, even just for a few moments? Let your list grow without any judgment. Items can be food-related, activity-related, TV or computer-related, the sky's the limit.

- Look at your list and check off the items that won't totally set you back or completely prevent you from reaching your goal. Cross off any remaining items that are too expensive or time-consuming, over-indulgent, or just over the top.

- Of the checked items, which one(s) might help you reach your goal, even if it takes you a little longer? Circle at least one item, or perhaps one item you can include in your daily schedule and one or two items you can include in your weekly or monthly schedule.

- Make a plan that includes when and how you will bring balance back to your life through adding these guilty pleasures. And, no need to feel guilty at all, because it's all part of the plan for being the best you.

DAY 8

LOOK FOR
OPPORTUNITIES

DO YOU EVER FEEL STUCK IN A RUT, like your life has become an endless routine of getting up, going to work at a job you don't necessarily enjoy, working long hours, coming home feeling too tired and burned out to make a healthy dinner and certainly having no energy left to engage with your family or pets, and the thought of working out or going for a walk never even crosses your mind? If so, congratulations, you are completely normal. Some might even call that living the American dream.

I've been there, and I'm sure most of you have been there as well. However, in order to keep a roof over our heads and food on the table, and hopefully provide some stability and consistency for our families, we do what we have to do, right? You may fantasize about yelling "I quit!" at your job, and even at your family or your life sometimes. I totally get it. We entered our adult lives feeling excited and special, and one day we wake up and realize that Burnout has become our new normal.

Burnout can look and feel different for everyone. For some, feeling exhausted, overwhelmed, and chronically stressed out can lead to frequent and fast anger when driving, and snapping at family members and pets. Some people end up being diagnosed with clinical depression or anxiety, or they suffer from insomnia. For me, when I finally noticed I was getting burned out, the worst symptom was… looking down and wondering when my belly started blocking the view of my feet. Yes, weight gain, especially in the stomach area, is a sign of chronic stress. When you're stressed, your body thinks you're in danger, so it holds on to every calorie you consume.

Many people, including myself for most of my adult life, live paycheck to paycheck. That's a huge burden, knowing that you are just one injury or illness or just one really bad day away from having your world come crashing down. You may feel like you cannot leave your unfulfilling job, and thus you are destined to keep doing what you're doing. You may still post on social media about fun events you attended, but is this the life you wanted, the life you dreamed of when you were little and thought you could do anything or be anything when you grew up?

Being both a psychotherapist and a massage therapist, pretty much everyone I talk to is "stressed out," "busy," or "tired," and sometimes "unmotivated," "overwhelmed," and "burned out." Those are currently the socially acceptable ways to respond when someone asks you how you're doing. However, if most people examined how they're truly feeling about themselves, their lives, jobs, situations and circumstances, it would probably be more accurate to respond with "unfulfilled," "unsatisfied," "lacking," "frustrated," "disappointed," and even "sad."

When we're being completely honest with ourselves, and reflecting on the all-too-common disconnect between our childhood dreams and our current lives…is that second set of words more truthful? Are you simply stressed out and busy, or is it more precise to say you are not really satisfied with your present life, and maybe you're missing the target you set for yourself many years ago? That sounds a bit depressing, I know, but I think that many people are in that same boat.

A while ago, I was feeling tired, overwhelmed, burned out, stretched to my limit. Whenever someone asked me how I was, I gave the common response, "busy." I wasn't living the life I wanted, and although it was initially hard for me to put into words, I was feeling empty, unfulfilled, and disappointed. In a few short years I was going to turn forty, and between my mental burnout and accompanying physical lethargy, I felt like I had one foot in the grave. Okay, that may be exaggerating slightly, but you get the picture. I was at a point in my life where I should've been living the dream, and I wasn't even close.

One day, I had enough. I was tired of feeling chronically burned out and overwhelmed with my unsatisfying routine that was sucking the life out of me and distancing me from my family. I needed to make some changes, fast. So what did I do? I started thinking about what makes me content and satisfied, motivated and excited to be alive. Personally, I feel content and satisfied when I'm helping people, when I know I'm making a significant difference in someone's life. I feel excited to be alive when I'm learning new things, when I'm being creative, challenged and active.

Realistically, I wasn't in a position to leave my job, nor did I necessarily want to. I was good at my job, and I worked hard to get the point I was at. It just wasn't something that I loved or that made me excited to get up in the morning. So how could I reconcile what I needed in my life with what I already had? How could I satisfy my intrinsic need to help others, while learning, creating and being challenged?

LOOK FOR OPPORTUNITIES

Knowing my specific needs, I started looking for educational opportunities. What workshops, courses, or programs were available where I could learn a challenging new skill, and use that skill to help people? What opportunities were out there that could push me to grow in new says, satisfy my need to work with people, and get me excited about life again?

You may be rolling your eyes, thinking that this tip isn't for you. Please continue reading, because this lesson can quickly take you from "surviving" to "thriving." You may be asking who has the time or energy to look for opportunities? YOU DO. And, it won't add to your burden or deplete what little energy you have left. In fact, it will very likely do the opposite.

You know what I found? Drum roll please… Massage school! At first the idea seemed so crazy. My family, although always supportive, was surprised when I first mentioned it. My colleagues and friends were startled and confused; they didn't understand why I would want to attend a trade school after already earning my doctorate degree and having a successful career. Being completely honest, I also thought the idea sounded a little outrageous initially, so I understood where everyone was coming from. The biggest question in my mind, was how on earth I was going to pull it all together, and P.S., was I really thinking clearly?

How could I fit a yearlong program, with 20 hours of classes, externship, and special events, plus a lengthy commute through rush hour traffic, into my busy life? I was already exhausted and mentally and emotionally unavailable for my family. And what was I going to do with my education, if I even made it to graduation…take on a second job? I had many questions, and not many answers. While I was pondering the idea, I toured the school, observed a class, brought my family to see the school and meet the admissions counselor, and applied for financial aid. While questioning everything, I continued to look for opportunities, and then more opportunities.

And then...I did it. I completed the full year of classes and externship and passed the state certification exam. Sure, I was tired after fighting rush hour traffic and usually had to take a short power nap in the backseat of my car before my evening classes, but that didn't matter because I was alive again. My life had meaning and purpose. I was being challenged in a way that was completely new to me. I was learning to help people using therapeutic touch, where before I helped people only through talking. The mind-body connection became crystal clear to me and I felt everything falling into place.

I loved massage school. Every single minute of it. Over the course of the year, whenever someone asked me how school was going, I LIT UP. My eyes sparkled, which people always commented on, and I immediately got energized just talking about it. Any questions by others or myself about whether this was a crazy idea were laid to rest.

I could probably fill an entire book with everything I learned about myself, others, and the world over the course of my year in massage school. It was nothing like any other school or program I've completed. If I'm going to be completely honest, I would say that year in massage school was the best year of my life.

And, it worked out in ways I didn't even imagine when I first started looking for opportunities, for something to help me escape burnout and get me out of my rut. Going back to school, even with the long hours and rush hour commute, gave me energy. My brain and body were both being challenged in completely new ways, and I was thriving. I met new people, amazing teachers and mentors that enriched my life, and I even started taking on private clients on the days I didn't have classes. And yes, I was still successfully maintaining my full-time job, and amazingly, my family was also thriving. Look for opportunities.

Many people questioned my sanity when I mentioned my schedule, but somehow it all came together. I was excited to get up each day, and I couldn't wait to go to class to see what new things I was going to learn. I was working harder than I ever had before, and each day was packed with work, school, homework, family. I was loving my life, and everyone around me could see how fun, exciting, and meaningful this was to me.

Through that year, I grew and changed and became excited about other opportunities. I started dreaming of having a private massage therapy practice. I did my research, looked for more opportunities, and guess what happened? I opened a small private practice exactly one month after I graduated. I didn't leave my full-time job, but my small practice brought me tremendous satisfaction because I was directly helping people, and I had the opportunity to create the business I wanted. I even started making my own line of hand-blended, all-natural products to sell at my private practice (and on my website).

One opportunity led to another, and none of this would have happened if I hadn't paused that one day a few years ago to really look at what was missing from my life, and what opportunities were available.

Now, let's take a look at your situation. Take a few minutes right now, and in your companion workbook or journal, write down how you're feeling. You may start with common responses, like "good," "busy," "stressed out," "overwhelmed," but then I want you to go deeper. How are you REALLY feeling? Look at your life, your current circumstances, and be honest with yourself. Are you doing the things you always thought you'd do someday? When you were sitting in elementary school, drawing a picture of what you wanted to be or do when you grew up, is that what you're doing right now? How are you REALLY feeling?

If you're completely satisfied with your circumstances, and you're living the life you always wanted, congratulations. If you do not fall into that category, you are probably in the majority, and you are in good company. If you just came to the conclusion that you're not only stressed out or overwhelmed, but also unfulfilled and dissatisfied with your current path, don't worry. You will be feeling better in no time. Look for opportunities.

Going back to school or learning a new career may not be the right thing for you right now. That's okay! The key is to first figure out what you value in life, what is important to you, what makes you tick, and when you feel excited to be alive. What has the potential to bring a sparkle to your eye? What energizes you?

Do you value helping people or animals? Maybe search for volunteer opportunities at a local hospital, community center, or animal shelter. Do you enjoy nature and like to go hiking or camping, but it's been years since you've gone? Look for a MeetUp group in your community that hikes and camps, or suggest an outing to co-workers, even if you've never socialized outside of work before.

Did you used to bake the most delicious cupcakes when you were younger, but haven't baked in forever? Look for a baking or decorating class, and see if there's any opportunities to sell your pastries. Figure out what makes you tick, what challenges you and helps you grow, what brings you joy and satisfaction. Then start looking online, talk to people in your neighborhood and at your job, and start looking for opportunities.

Do you feel like you don't have time to look for opportunities, or the bandwidth to even think about what interests you? At the same time, do you find yourself sitting in front of the TV in the evenings, or binge-watching Netflix shows on the weekends? Do you scroll through your social media accounts as soon as your eyes open in the morning, on every break at work, during the commercials of your evening TV shows, and even when you use the restroom?

We think TV and games and social media apps will bring us relaxation and relief from burnout, but it doesn't usually work like that. Adding screen time to your daily schedule, particularly when you fill every spare minute with it, can add stress to your life and distract you from what is truly meaningful and valuable to you. If you believe that TV or video games or social media makes you feel happier, more satisfied with your life, and excited to wake up in the morning, I'm going to ask you to do an experiment. If you tend to check your social media accounts during every spare second, I want you to do this experiment. If you find yourself watching TV every evening, or binge-watching shows on the weekends to relax, please do this experiment. You may want to sit down to hear about the experiment, because you might not like it.

I recommend that you take a tech vacation for at least five days, but preferably seven so you can include a whole weekend. You can still keep your phone and text messaging turned on in case family, friends or work needs to reach you (for an EMERGENCY), but please turn off the notifications on all your social media accounts. Leave your television turned off for the entire week. Don't play any video games or games on your phone. You might think I'm trying to torture you but I'm willing to bet that this will be the best week you've had in a long time. So what will you do instead of staring at a screen?

You will use the time to think about YOU. Explore what energizes you, what you value, what brings you joy. Take a walk, without music, and think about these things. Write in your companion workbook or journal (and please review the Action Items and workbook prior to starting your tech vacation, for additional guidance). Find inspiration as you look up (and ease your tech neck) and see what's going on in the world around you. Go outside, engage your muscles, just see what comes to mind when you're disconnected from technology.

As things start coming to mind that interest and excite you, and I know they will, write them down. At the end of your tech vacation, first examine how you're feeling. How was it for you to unplug for a week? Are you still mad at me, or was it better than you ever imagined? Now look at the list you created and start looking for opportunities related to those things. Do research online, talk to your friends and colleagues, send email inquiries.

Track your progress, and within a few days, choose an opportunity on your list and go for it. It could be something relatively small that takes an hour or a day to complete, or it could be something larger that requires a commitment on your part, such as going to school or learning a new trade. Even though you're technically adding to your life, you will feel so much better, especially if you are doing an activity that reflects your values while also bringing you enjoyment.

THINKING POINTS:

- Consider your current routine and circumstances, and how you feel about your work and day-to-day life.

- Are you experiencing burnout? How do you know? What does burnout feel like for you?

- If you are feeling burned out, how long have you been feeling burned out, and would you say it's mild, moderate, or severe?

- Start thinking about topics that interest you, based on your values. What do you want to learn more about, that will enrich your life, be meaningful, and allow you to grow and be challenged?

- What excites you, energizes you, makes you feel alive?

ACTION ITEMS:

- On a scale of 1-10, with 1 being no burnout and 10 being so burned out you're ready to quit everything, how would you rate your current level of burnout? Please write it down.

- If you're planning to take a tech vacation, the remaining items can be done throughout your break.

- Write down a list of things that you value, or find meaningful. For example, is it important to you to help people, rescue animals, or protect the natural resources on our planet?

- Write down a list of topics that interest you, inspire you, and excite you. Just let the ideas flow onto your paper without judgment or concern.

- Place checkmarks by three topics that interest you the most, that are also aligned with the values on your first list.

- Spend time looking for opportunities that are available related to them. Can you read some articles online, locate a workshop or course to learn more, or talk to someone who knows about the topic?

- Select one thing you want to focus on, and look for a variety of opportunities available locally, online, and at a distance. Note the costs, time requirements, and start making your plans. Go for it!!

- You may be having too much fun to remember this last item, but if you think of it, after pursuing opportunities related to your interest, revisit the idea of burnout, and note your level of burnout on the same 1-10 scale. Has your number dropped? Even if you are still at the same job, and you added things to your schedule, are you feeling better? Remember, look for opportunities throughout your life that reflect your values and make you tick, and even if you aren't able to do them full-time, you will still be living your best life.

DO IT ANYWAY

I RECENTLY WASN'T FEELING WELL, AND BY THE third day in a row of being under the weather, I was on the mend but decided to stay home from work for one day to rest and recover.

Before I started my sick day, I drove in to work very early to call my clients and get a few urgent things done, and I was back at home by 9am. I immediately crawled into bed and fell asleep, with plans to sleep as long as possible. I fantasized about spending the entire day in bed, doing nothing but sleeping, reading, and watching television. Sounds so luxurious, right? I think we all dream of having a whole day in bed, to just be away from the world, cozy and still.

Well, I awoke a measly hour later, and I was already feeling better. I watched the rest of the Today Show on NBC, a show I've loved since I was little but can only watch on sick or vacation days. That show ended at 11am, and then…the battle started. The internal debate in my mind that happens when I feel like I'm wasting precious time. "I'm missing out on a beautiful day." "I should get up. My body is going to be stiff and my neck will hurt tomorrow." "I am still feeling ill off and on. I should stay in bed and just try hard to sleep and rest all day." "I'm not that sick. I can get a couple things done around the house." "I should go pick up a few groceries and take advantage of the quiet streets and stores." "My son's at home on summer break, I should surprise him and take him to Starbucks." "I should stay in bed and complete my online trainings that are soon due." "Just try to sleep some more, your body needs it." "For the love of God, get up and do something!" AHHHHH!!!!

Those were literally the thoughts bouncing around my head, tormenting me endlessly while I laid there "resting." So, being the logical person that I am, I first assessed how I was feeling physically, and at the moment I was feeling okay. I got out of bed, found my son, and asked him to go to the store with me to get a few things. I wasn't feeling incredibly strong, and I knew I had to buy a case of water, so I figured I'd use him for his muscles and then reward him with Starbucks. Brilliant, right?

We went, and I was fine. Better than fine. I bought my groceries, which had been burdening me since I started feeling ill a few days ago. After we got home, I laid down on my bed with my laptop, and completed an online training. I felt quite accomplished after that, because the training took much less time than I had anticipated. So, check sleep off my list, check groceries off my list, check make my son happy off my list, check complete required training off my list. By 1pm on my sick day, I was feeling like I had accomplished a lot.

After my initial happiness from feeling accomplished wore off, I realized that I was not feeling well, kind of weak and under the weather again. I hadn't eaten anything since 7:30am, so I went and got some saltine crackers. I laid back down, ate the saltines, and started watching some more training webinars that were coming due. Those webinars had been weighing on me for the past couple of weeks, a constant invisible burden. I was tired of thinking about them and worrying about them, so I finally completed them, even though I was taking a sick day. I was caught up, I learned a lot, and the weight was lifted. Hooray!

Then, after that excitement, I took a nap for probably another hour, ate a light dinner, rested again for another hour, then got up and went for a 1-mile walk. I struggled to get out the door to start that walk, and I left about 45 minutes later than usual, but I did it. I woke up the next day feeling completely normal and healthy and back to my regular life.

What is my purpose in telling you all about my sick day? To fascinate you with my exciting life? Nope. My point is to share my struggle, the internal battle that happens when I want or need to do something, but I don't feel like doing it.

There may be many times in your life, perhaps even many times throughout each day, when you want or need to do something, but you don't feel like doing it. So, you go along with your feelings, and then you end up regretting your decision.

You want to be fit, but you don't feel like taking a walk after dinner, so you sit in front of the television, probably beating yourself up for being "lazy." Going out with friends sounds fun, but yet you don't really feel like it, so you stay home, possibly feeling disappointed for missing out on a good time. You told yourself you were going to take a walk on your lunch break, but then you don't feel like leaving your chair, so you eat at your desk while scrolling through your phone, and then you feel lousy for the rest of the day. You set a goal to do more active family activities, but then you don't feel like playing soccer with your kids at the park, so you all stay home and watch a movie, while you regret that decision for the entire length of the movie. (I can feel some of you nodding along as you read this).

DO IT ANYWAY

Sounds so simple, right? This is an "easy to say, harder to do" lesson, so let's break it down. If you understand the rationale, I believe you will be motivated and ready to give it a try.

First, I want to tell you something about your feelings, specifically the "I don't feel like it" feelings. Please don't take this the wrong way, but they don't matter. Our feelings pass faster than a cloud in the sky, and while every feeling is valid, you certainly shouldn't plan your day around a passing "I don't feel like it" feeling, or let that feeling convince you to not do something you need or want to do. DO IT ANYWAY.

You can feel like you don't want to do something, AND you can still do it. In case you've never tried ignoring that "I don't feel like it" feeling, I'm going to let you in on a little secret. If you ignore that feeling, and follow through with your plans, the good feelings will follow. You may not feel like a million bucks, but you will very likely feel accomplished, satisfied, and perhaps proud or even happy. Odds are you will not regret following through with what you wanted or needed to do.

Even if you don't feel like doing something, do it anyway, and you will be glad you did. It's rare to hear someone say they regretted taking a walk, or playing soccer with their kids in the park, or going hiking or out with friends. Alternately, I have heard people say they regretted not doing things that they had been wanting or planning to do.

Follow through, do it anyway, and the good feelings will follow. No matter how cranky, irritable, heavy or blah you feel, still do whatever it is you need to do. Get up and make your bed, brush your teeth, put your dishes in the dishwasher, take a walk, cut up an apple so you have it ready for snack time. You will feel much better afterwards.

The hardest times during my sick day were when I was laying there in bed, arguing with myself about what I should be doing but didn't feel like doing, and feeling cranky the whole time. When I finally ignored my feelings and followed through with what I wanted to do, I felt a thousand times better. Not only was my crankiness gone, but I didn't have to add regret on top of crankiness.

In case you're still not on board, and maybe listening to that "I don't feel like it" feeling is so engrained in you that it's going to take more to convince you to disregard it, that's okay. Just stay with me, and keep reading with an open mind.

Think of something that you need or want to get done today, and please choose a task that you don't really feel like doing. Now, take a minute and think about any risks that might be involved in doing it anyway. This is something you need to get done today, and perhaps you are arguing with yourself about how you should do it but you don't wanna do it (insert whiney voice here). What are you risking if you do it anyway? Will you get behind on social media? Miss your favorite show on TV? Lose those last 15 minutes of hitting your snooze button?

It's possible that you have some valid concerns about potential risks. Losing sleep or expending too much energy, for example, could be issues if you have certain health problems. However, there are usually workarounds, and I encourage you to consider planning your activities or tasks for times that fit with your body's schedule, and not around feelings of "I don't feel like it." I'm guessing that the majority of you don't have many, if any, valid risks to consider.

Now take some time to think through the benefits of doing it anyway, of following through with what you need or want to do regardless of your feelings. What good will come from doing whatever it is you "should" do today? Depending on what you're considering doing, some benefits that immediately come to my mind include getting physical activity, laughing with friends, bonding with family, breathing fresh air, renewing of body and mind, reducing stress, laughing and having fun. What comes to your mind?

Which list is longer? Which was easier to write? Take another look at your lists, and determine if the benefits outweigh the risks. (Are you feeling a little more prepared to give this lesson a try?)

Finally, start adding tasks to your calendar. Having things officially scheduled can be helpful if you struggle with "I don't feel like it" feelings. You may have heard about the importance of scheduling your workouts on your calendar just like you would a medical appointment, so that you take it seriously and show up no matter what. The same sentiment goes for everything else you need or want to do. You can schedule everyday tasks such as wash dishes, buy groceries, fold the laundry and vacuum the house. This may feel silly at first, but it helps. I've even been known to have my shower scheduled on my calendar. (Seriously!) If you worry about having enough energy to get things done, and I can totally understand that, split your tasks throughout the week and across the month.

I personally do most of my housecleaning on Saturdays, but I sometimes do laundry and a few other things during the week so that my entire Saturday isn't taken up with chores. If I know I have plans on a Saturday, I will move my chores to other days, and schedule them throughout the week in my calendar in a manner that is most appealing to me. If you create lists that are too long and burdensome, they will likely be harder to complete, so keep them short and simple.

Be sure to also add pleasurable activities to your calendar. That way you will have a more balanced perspective of your life when you look at your schedule. Pleasurable activities can be something as inexpensive and casual as going for a walk or soaking in a bubble bath. Or, you can go to a matinee movie right after work one day, or grab some light take-out on your way home from work and stop by a park where you can spread out a blanket and eat and read for a while before heading home to start your evening.

Always have activities (including chores, tasks, and pleasurable events) planned in your calendar, and then no matter how you feel, do them anything. No need to waste a single minute arguing with yourself. And, don't back out of the fun things you have planned, even if your list of excuses is a mile long. Make your lists of risks and benefits if you need to, and then get to it.

THINKING POINTS:

- Do you ever battle with yourself in your mind, where part of you wants to stay still and part of you wants to do something?

- What does that argument sound like? What are the reasons you don't want to do something? Is it because you "don't feel like it?" Which part usually wins?

- How often do you face this dilemma? How does it make you feel?

- The next time you have this internal battle, ask yourself what you are risking, if you ignore your feelings and do it anyway. Anything at all? What are the benefits to doing it anyway?

ACTION ITEMS:

- What do you need to do? Have you been putting off something that needs done? What do you want to do? An activity with your friends, family, or by yourself?

- Ignore your "I don't feel like it" feelings, and do it anyway. Right now, if possible. Go do whatever it is you need or want to do, whatever has been burdening you. Then come back and go on to the next item.

- Immediately after you complete your task, write down what you did and how you feel. Did anything negative come from doing the task? Anything positive? Let this serve as evidence, as a reminder, for the next time you are faced with the internal dilemma of staying still versus doing it anyway.

- Experiment with this concept. When you feel that internal battle starting, try giving in and staying still. How do you feel and what was the outcome? Then try pushing through and doing it anyway, and re-evaluate how you feel. Notice any differences?

- When you are struggling, list the risks and benefits to doing it anyway. You can write them down or do them in your head, whatever works best. Weigh the evidence and make a decision.

- Schedule your tasks, including things that need done and things you want to do, on your calendar. Spread chores and activities out across the week and month based on work or sleep schedules or other competing priorities. And, no matter how you feel, do the tasks when they are planned.

DAY 10

BE A DREAMER

I GREW UP ON ABOUT TEN ACRES OF land in Lancaster County, PA. Except for a few acres of green grass that made up our front and side yards, the land was mostly covered by trees. We were pretty isolated, with no neighbors in sight, no sidewalks, no cable television. I didn't appreciate the remoteness of the location at the time, although I do long for it now on days when I get fed up with always being surrounded by people. It was amazingly beautiful, breathtaking, and peaceful.

The best part of growing up in the woods was the creek that ran from one side of the property to the other, crossing right in front of our house. It entered from beyond the side yard, then flowed through the front yard, creating a twinkling barrier between the house and the front yard. When it rained, the creek became quite full, but normally it was calm and pleasant, maintaining around 4-6 inches of flowing water.

As a child, I always wanted a special place where I could be alone to daydream about my future. When I was very little, I tried to turn my bedroom closet into my special, private dreaming place. I put a little chair in there under my clothes and took in my books and blankets. I made a good effort, but it was usually dark under the clothes even with the light on, and it was a bit claustrophobic.

When I got a little older, maybe mid-elementary school age, I fantasized about having a tree house. Man, I wanted a tree house so bad! I even drew up the plans for an original tree house one day and handed it in with my homework to one of my teachers. I walked around our property countless times, examining trees, and pitched the idea tirelessly to my parents. I never got a tree house, and as a parent now, I certainly can't blame them.

When I was a teenager, I was still a total dreamer, probably even more so than when I was younger. My dad understood that, and he built me a bridge across our creek, at the back part of our property that was quiet and private. My own bridge! Technically anyone could walk across the bridge, but no one ever did because it didn't really lead anywhere. The special part of the bridge, was the bridge itself. My dad knew I needed my own space, and it was perfect. I used to take my notebook and pen out there, and sometimes a snack because I knew I'd be there for a while. I loved it so much!

I'd usually start my bridge time laying on my back, looking up at the sky. There were big trees all around that blocked any direct light, but the sun filtered down through the rustling leaves. The creek flowed under me. Looking back, I can say without a doubt that for me, that was the most peaceful place in the world. The swaying trees, rustling leaves, sparkling sunshine, gentle creek, chirping birds, and otherwise silence… I was totally safe, and at peace. There was nothing to harm me there. Not teenage stress, anxiety, peer pressure, negative body image. Anything was possible on my safe and magical bridge.

Eventually I would roll over and start writing, usually making lists of goals or plans, dreaming and fantasizing about my future. I thought about potential relationships, kids, traveling, future education, friends, my family, jobs and careers, God and my place in the world.

I always felt so small, laying there under those big trees, listening to the captivating creek beneath me. And my dreams always felt so big. I would wonder, were my dreams too big? Did I deserve to have them? Should I aim smaller? Would I ever have the courage to leave home and follow my dreams? Would my family feel sad if I left? What if I failed? Louder than these questions, however, was my excitement, my faith, my hope, and my belief that anything was possible.

Years passed, and the days of dreaming on my bridge ended. As adult and parental responsibilities took over my life, and my schedule became packed with school and work, I let go of one of the most important pieces of me - the part that used to lose track of time while daydreaming about my future. Why did that matter? Turns out that without that part of me, I tended to get stuck in an endless pattern of prioritizing everyone else's needs and wishes above my own, because I didn't have my own desires. In that space, I wasn't living my best life or feeling particularly well, and those around me weren't seeing the best version of me.

After feeling stagnant for a long time, I thankfully realized what was missing, and started giving myself space and time to dream and fantasize about the possibilities for my life and my future. It felt strange at first, and I struggled with feeling a bit guilty, worried about being indulgent or self-serving. However, the light came back on in my life, heart, and mind. I felt excited, curious, creative, and more accessible and helpful to those around me.

Today, I am always looking for a tree to lay under, or for a bridge to sit on. Sometimes, when I'm feeling stressed out from a hectic day or just from being so close to people all the time, I get almost obsessive about finding a tree. Luckily (and amusingly), my wife has made it her mission to find me parks with nice trees, and to point out perfect trees when we're out driving. It's nearly impossible to find privacy and quiet, even in nature areas, in the San Francisco Bay Area. I don't think the peace of my childhood actually exists out here, or perhaps it just doesn't exist in my adult world. But I still yearn for it. And more importantly, I recognize the importance of taking that time and space for myself.

BE A DREAMER

Human beings have the unique ability to dream about the future. It's an amazing gift that can richly enhance our lives and open our minds and hearts to all that might be possible. Children are instinctively dreamers, and we witness them testing out possibilities through their creative and imaginative role plays, dress-up times, and drawings. Teenagers are the original daydreamers, letting their minds wander and create, sometimes when they are supposed to be focusing in school. Soon after high school, most people start focusing on work, college, paying the bills, or starting a family, and the hours of getting lost in thought are quickly filled by new priorities. And, along with the shift in focus and new responsibilities, comes those ever present feelings of being stressed out, burned out, and tired.

When we dream, when we fantasize about our future and get lost in the possibilities, dormant parts of us wake up and we feel more alive. Can you remember what it was like when you were younger, perhaps a child or teenager, and you let your imagination run wild? Maybe you fantasized about what you wanted to be when you grew up, a certain love interest, the hot cars you were going to own or all the kids you wanted to have someday. What did you dream about? No doubt your dream time now will look and feel very different from your earlier years, but sometimes reflecting back can help your creative juices start flowing.

You can dream about tomorrow or next week, maybe six months from now or even five or ten years from now. Step outside of your day to day life and consider the possibilities of what could be. If it's been a while since you let your mind wander in this way, I encourage you to just relax and be open to whatever comes up. This is a safe and fun time, so if worries or concerns start crowding your mind, gently redirect back to the purpose of this moment. You can write down your thoughts, draw pictures, create poetry, or just let your eyes glaze over as your imagination flows. This isn't the time to write out a detailed goal plan, but is instead an opportunity to let your mind wander as it pleases.

Sometimes I go to a park near my house, and even though there are kids nearby playing basketball and parents walking past with their kids in strollers, I spread out a blanket under a special tree that reminds me of my childhood in the way the sunlight filters through its branches. And I dream. Other days I go to the beach to watch the waves. Since childhood, moving water has always inspired me and healed me, whether it's a creek, river, or ocean. Any issues I'm dealing with quickly lose their power, and I'm renewed as I fill my lungs with the fresh air that can only be found by moving water.

Where can you go to dream? Was there a place you used to go when you were younger, where you could be alone and let your imagination roam freely? Whether or not you had a childhood space like that, can you create a space like that today? Never worry about what others might think, if they see you laying on a blanket under a tree somewhere while they are hurrying by…if you listen closely, you can hear them murmuring their envy, that they wish they were in your place. Can you make time to be alone and dream about your future? The possibilities for your amazing and wonderful life?

When I'm at home, looking around and seeing things that need done, or hearing my son playing his loud music, or when I'm negotiating traffic and running errands, I'm not in the mental space to dream about my future. Dreaming cannot be multitasked! Designate a time and space, and don't let anything interfere. Approach your dreaming time as a commitment that cannot be canceled. It's not selfish and it's not a luxury. It's part of living your life, of being the best you that you can possibly be.

What do you need in your dreaming place? Where will you find peace, safety, restoration, inspiration? Do you need trees? Moving water? Quiet and stillness? Or do you envision yourself sitting on a bench in a park, surrounded by laughing children? Perhaps relaxing at an outdoor café in the middle of a bustling city? Making yourself comfortable in front of a painting in an art gallery? Sitting on the beach, toes in the sand, watching the waves?

You may think you don't have time to dream, but if you make this a priority, you will find the time. You don't need a certain number of hours each week or each month to benefit, and it's fine to start small if your schedule is super-packed at the moment, or if you're having some hesitation. Find at least 30 minutes at a time, even just once or twice a month if that's all you can spare initially. I have a feeling you will start increasing your time, once you start seeing and feeling the results.

Try not to end your dreaming sessions suddenly. Take a few minutes to reflect on your time, on how your thoughts flowed, and notice if you learned anything about yourself. There's no judgment when you're dreaming, or during your time of reflection. Just let your mind wander and imagine the possibilities. You may be surprised at what comes up for you when you make time to dream.

At the end of your special time, notice how you feel as you're packing up your blanket, leaving the café, or heading back to your car from the beach. Is there a lightness in your step, a twinkle in your eye, an excitement in your heart? Something magical happens when we daydream, when we allow ourselves to be open and free. I think it's a reawakening of our spirits, a glimpse at our souls. If it's been a long time since you experienced this, I encourage you to give it a try. Be a dreamer.

THINKING POINTS:

- When was the last time you allowed yourself to be a dreamer? Do you see the potential value in dreaming?

- Think about what you might enjoy or need in your dreaming place...water, fresh air, children or people, calmness or activity? What makes you feel comfortable and relaxed?

- Start thinking of places that would work for you, and when you can fit this time into your schedule.

ACTION ITEMS:

- Make a list of possibilities for your dreaming places. Your list can include places from your past, places you've never been to, places far away or just down the street.

- Look over your list, and note which options you could work with right now. Are any of the options close to your home? If not, could any of the options be adapted to where you currently are? Select one or two options that you can explore now.

- Schedule a time to go to the space you selected as the closest and easiest option. It may not be your ideal place to dream, but it will work for now and will give you a taste of the possibilities. Set aside at least 30 minutes, and take along whatever you need (e.g., workbook, paper, pens or markers, water and snacks).

- Don't set an agenda or any limits at all for yourself during your dreaming time. Just enjoy your surroundings and your time, and start dreaming, thinking, fantasizing, and contemplating.

- As your time comes to a close, reflect on what came up for you, and how you're feeling.

- After you start allowing yourself time to dream and become more comfortable with the concept, look back over your list of potential dreaming spots. Can you make a plan to visit another location? Maybe even plan a day trip or a vacation that includes one of your most peaceful and ideal locations?

DAY 11

APPRECIATE YOUR BODY

WHEN I WAS IN EARLY ELEMENTARY SCHOOL, SOMEWHERE between second and fourth grade, I started worrying about my body. We had magazines like *Shape* and *Fitness* around the house, and I read every one. I also became interested in those other teenage magazines that tell you what your body should look like, how you need to look and act to attract attention, and how you should dress, style your hair, and apply your make-up.

I couldn't get enough of those magazines. At the time, I probably thought that I liked those magazines, and that I enjoyed reading them. But looking back, I can see that I developed an unhealthy obsession with comparing my body to the bodies in the magazines, and there was no real enjoyment taking place. At the time, around age 8, I quickly realized that I was not thin enough, pretty enough, strong enough... simply not good enough.

I remember asking for the "Get in Shape Girl" set one year for Christmas, when I was still in elementary school. This was back in the '80's, and it included a lightweight set of dumbbells, a cassette with music and instruction, and legwarmers. (Yes, the legwarmers were the best part.) I thought, after reading those magazines, that I really needed to tone up, and this was going to help me.

I did that routine faithfully, but soon I sadly realized I was not looking at all like those girls in the magazines. I didn't understand, and I was frustrated. My body was not turning into the beautiful, thin, perfect body that I envisioned and desired.

Junior high did little to improve my body image. I have a clear memory of walking into my 7th grade social studies class, and one of my male classmates, who had never spoken to me before, told me I had a big butt. After that, I started obsessively checking out my rear view in the mirror before leaving my house, trying to see what everyone else would see. Looking back from my adult perspective, I feel sorry for my 7th grade self. Although I was going through my awkward puberty stage, I was actually slender, and that kid was just rude.

I can't say that I was the only one in my household who was overly focused on size, shape and weight. When I was in high school, my whole family, including my mother, father, sister and me, had weekly weigh-ins every Tuesday morning. We would all work hard throughout the week to eat as healthfully as we could and work out as much as we could, and then wake up early Tuesday morning in hopes of losing the most weight out of the whole family. The "winner" didn't get anything tangible, but that person still felt good knowing they were the most successful that week.

At the time, I was in my mid-teens. I was 5'6" tall, and I weighed 115-120 pounds. Keep in mind, for a 5'6" woman, it's ideal to weigh approximately 125-145 pounds. I remember having my fat measured at the high school weight room, and although their calipers test probably wasn't 100% accurate, they told me I had 12% body fat. And I still thought I was fat. And ugly, and undesirable. My thighs were too wiggly, my butt too big, my feet too big (not that I could even change them), my stomach stuck out the front and my butt stuck out the back. I was a mess, clearly.

Some weeks, at our family weigh-in I would drop a pound or two. I was happy for a moment, until I reminded myself that I needed to lose more. Maybe I could get down to 110 if I really tried harder. Then I would look better and feel better and be prettier and more attractive and more desirable. But it was never enough. I never lost enough weight to start feeling better about myself and my body.

When I look back at pictures of myself in high school, I was thin. I wasn't painfully thin or fragile-looking, but I was undeniably thin. I remember buying jeans in size 2 and feeling bad that I couldn't buy size 0, the smallest size available. Darn it, if I could just lose a few more pounds, size 0 might be within my reach. And I felt bad about myself.

I feel sad for the teenage me. And the even sadder thing is, I don't think my story is all that different from teenagers in general, past or present. Maybe most children don't become obsessed with fitness magazines quite as early as me, and no doubt most families don't have weekly weigh-ins, but I do believe that children internalize very early that they aren't thin enough, pretty enough, fit enough, strong enough, muscular enough, curvy enough…never good enough.

If anything, it may be worse today than it was when I was younger. In the age of social media, teens (and many adults) feel pressured to post perfect pictures on Facebook and Snapchat and Instagram, and they spend countless hours watching tutorials on YouTube on how to apply make-up, how to work out and how to get the perfect angle of the camera so they can look perfect in selfies. Teenage magazines aren't popular any longer because teens can just look at their phones to see the latest pics of their favorite star, taken approximately 5 minutes ago. We are constantly being bombarded with social media evidence that confirms we are never good enough.

When I was in my late 30's, I went through a mini crisis and thought I was starting to look old. I had noticed a few fine lines starting, my pores looked larger, and I didn't have the glow that I wanted in my face. So, I spent a ton of money on a set of high-end products created for women exactly like me (i.e., in crisis and willing to spend a lot of dough to feel better).

These products promised me beauty, youth, no more lines, smaller pores, basically a new and younger, more perfect, me. I sit here chuckling as I write this, because it probably goes without saying that those expensive products didn't do a darn thing for my skin. And unfortunately I think that chunk of money is still sitting on my credit card.

After spending that much money on products that did not turn back the clock, I started examining myself and the messages I was telling myself. Now, this did not happen overnight. You can't change thirty years of reinforced thinking in a week or two. But, I slowly started to realize that my body is nothing short of a miracle.

Fine lines and large pores are truly meaningless, when I look at the body that gave me healthy childhood and teenage years, that birthed a child, that fought hard to save my life when I was a young mother and had complications related to appendicitis, that kept me going through thirteen years of college, that fought once again to save my life in my early 30's when I had emergency surgery and internal bleeding, and that to this day allows me to live independently and generally free from pain and suffering. I mean, wow, right? That's a pretty incredible body I have. Who am I to criticize this amazing vessel I've been blessed with?

APPRECIATE YOUR BODY

As a massage therapist, I've seen a lot of bodies. I can tell you without hesitation that everyone has very different bodies. And, no one's body looks like those bodies I used to strive for in the fitness or teen magazines. Can you believe that? I thought those were the standards, the norm from which I was falling short. Turns out that's not the case. Real people, lovely and amazing people, have "extra" weight all over their bodies, have dimples, stretch marks, wrinkles, scars, varicose veins, patches of hair here and there, dry feet, little rolls here, big rolls there, and some are very thin with seemingly nothing but skin and bones. And you know what? They are all beautiful and perfect.

Let me say that again, because I really want you to hear it. Every body is beautiful and perfect, as they are today. When I give someone a massage, it never crosses my mind to judge them or to use the standards that I used to place on myself. I see their muscles working hard to hold up their bodies to get them through their day, their necks bending and hurting from holding up their physical and emotional pain, their posture sometimes paying the price of a lifetime of stress. In every body that I touch, I see strength. I see vitality. I see the overcoming of pain, and the desire to feel better. Appreciate your body.

This could be the hardest lesson for some people reading this book, and depending on the day, I still struggle with this. We can't escape the constant messages we receive from advertisements, magazines and social media, trying to tell us we're not good enough. But please, hear me out. Your body is perfect, absolutely perfect, right now, today. You may not believe me yet, but I hope that you will very soon.

There are things you can do today, and every day, to help you appreciate the body you have. Some suggestions may feel uncomfortable initially, but please don't disregard an idea based on the chance that you might experience a mildly unpleasant feeling.

One thing you can do each evening is mindfully self-massage your arms and hands, legs and feet. It's nice to use lotion, but you don't have to. Really take your time, and as you're massaging, silently thank that part of your body for helping to get you through your day. Appreciate it's strength and stamina, with no judgement attached. Take several minutes on each body part and notice your skin and muscles, the strength and vitality in those parts. P.S. Add a nice scalp massage at the end, and you will be all set for a good night's sleep.

Doing self-massage may feel strange initially, especially if you are not used to caring for your body in a loving manner. If massaging your hands and feet with your own hands is too uncomfortable, try rolling your feet on a tennis ball, and just squeezing the ball with your hands. Once your hands and feet are used to being touched, switch to a hands-on, more assertive approach. Specifically, do compressions on your feet with your hands. Just grasp them firmly, all over, from your heels to your toes and back to your heels. Then squeeze each hand with the opposite hand. Compress each finger and all around your hand. I'm guessing you will end up loving this. Finally, when you're ready, try using lotion and a gentler, more soothing touch. Take as long as you need to work through this process. Appreciate your body.

Another way to appreciate your body is to simply accept your entire body, every single part of it, exactly as it is today. Period. I'm pretty sure we all have body parts that we've disliked for many years, even decades. Odds are, those body parts are not going to go away or radically change any time soon. So, accept them. Look at your body in the mirror, clothed or unclothed, and starting at the top of your body, tell yourself (out loud if possible) that you accept your head, eyes, nose, etc., etc.

You don't need to necessarily name every single body part, but definitely include all parts that you have been rejecting or ignoring. You may find yourself feeling embarrassed or even blushing – that's okay, keep going! Try to do this each time you use the restroom, but maybe do it silently if you're in a public restroom…up to you!

Your whole body works together to support you and keep you well, so please take time to recognize it and accept it. It's okay if you don't immediately fall in love with a body part you've been disliking for a long time, but do take the time to affirm what it does for you, it's role in keeping you alive, active, healthy or whole, and appreciate it.

Keep doing this, every chance you get. Maybe, just maybe, even give yourself a little smile in the mirror sometimes.

If you really struggle with this, please don't worry or give up. Literally, try this exercise for 30 seconds a day, just really quick and you're done. Start by acknowledging a body part that you already accept. If you like or even just accept your eyes, tell them you like them and accept them. When you get to a body part you don't like, just say hello and then continue on to another part that you already accept. Come back to that part tomorrow and say hello again.

By next week you may be able to add a "how's it going" when you get to that body part, or even a "hey, just stopping to say hello again." You get my point. If this is extra challenging, start small, simply acknowledge, and do what you can. Odds are you have rejected certain body parts or possibly your entire body for years, decades, or even a lifetime, and that's not something to resolve overnight or in a week or two. Eventually you will find yourself becoming more comfortable with your body, until you can fully accept it.

Once you are able to accept body parts that you used to dislike, start enjoying them. You will get to this point! I have body parts and features that I wasted thirty years rejecting, and to what end? I still have them, and honestly, no one but me has ever given a darn about them. I'm at the point where I can even say they are part of what makes me unique and special.

I know, beyond a shadow of a doubt, that your body is amazing and wonderful, right now, today, and you will never convince me otherwise. I'm guessing there's a part of you that wants to believe me, that maybe you really are okay. The truth is, you are more than okay. Start appreciating your body by taking care of it in a loving and mindful way. Accept your body, over and over again, until you believe it in your head and heart. Don't worry, just keep working on this, and soon you will get a glimpse at what it feels like to not only accept your body, but to embrace and wholeheartedly love your amazing body.

THINKING POINTS:

- Take time to reflect on how you view your body. What are your core beliefs about your body? What views did you internalize as a young child, teenager, and young adult?

- Have your views changed over time?

- Do you hear a negative voice in your mind about your body? If yes, who do you hear? A parent, sibling, bully, teacher? Or did you internalize beliefs from looking at magazines, TV, or the internet?

- Do you already appreciate your body, or accept parts of your body? What do you like or accept about yourself? Do you do anything to acknowledge those parts?

ACTION ITEMS:

- Write down a list of things you dislike about your body, then a list of things you like about your body. Which list is longer? Do you "believe" one side more than the other?

- Practice the self-massage routine described in this chapter every day for the next 30 days. Massage your hands and feet, using a tennis ball, compressions, or lotion, whatever is most accessible for you. Make a checkmark in your workbook each day you do it.

- Tonight, when you are getting ready for bed, practice the acceptance routine described in this chapter. Take it slow, and start wherever you're at, even if that means simply saying hello to a body part you dislike or usually ignore. Do this every time you use the restroom for the next 30 days.

- After 30 days, make new lists of what you dislike and like about your body. Cover up your first list – don't simply copy the lists! When you're done, compare the lists. Has anything disappeared from the dislike list? Have any of your dislikes moved to the likes list? Continue for another 30 days, and check your lists again. Keep at it, and you will see progress.

TAKE A RISK

MY DAD WAS 45-YEARS-OLD WHEN I WAS BORN. He was older than any of my friends' dads, and almost twenty years older than my mom. His parents had lived to be quite old, into their nineties, and I thought my dad was going to be around forever. He was always active and healthy and young at heart. He retired when I was still in high school, and sadly, soon after he retired, he developed breathing problems that ultimately incapacitated him and took his life a few days after he turned seventy.

I was twenty-five when he died, and my son was just a couple weeks shy of his first birthday. I'm glad I had my dad around for my childhood years, and I'm happy that he was able to meet my son and feel assured that we were going to be okay and have good lives. And, I wish he had been around to be a part of everything that's happened in the past fifteen years.

My dad regularly shows up in my dreams, as recently as a couple nights ago. In my dreams, he's always standing tall and strong and healthy, walking beside me, never sick or in a wheelchair. In this recent dream, we were walking in the town where I had lived in Pennsylvania for the twelve years prior to moving to California. The town didn't look the same, as dreams tend to distort places, but he was the same as always. Loving, supportive, quiet, just walking beside me through the town. We got to a part of the road that dropped off so steeply that I was afraid to continue, and he went first and helped me. I felt peaceful when I woke up in the morning, thankful for that time I had with my dad even if it was in my dream.

One thing that I learned from my dad's illness and early passing, is that we are never promised tomorrow. We are not guaranteed a long and healthy life, free of struggles or hardships. We are always just one phone call or doctor's visit away from being brought to our knees, from having our lives suddenly going in a different direction than we ever wanted or expected. We don't ever know how much time we have left.

From the time I was little, I was a dreamer, always looking towards my future and often getting swept away by goals and fantasies. While it was fun, and I would argue that every child should dream big and often, I also don't have many memories of my growing up years, including memories of my dad. I was always so busy thinking of what was to come, that I forgot to pay attention to what was happening in the moment. After my dad's passing, I realized that I needed to be more present, to live in the here and now, to make memories of today. Yet, I'm still a dreamer at heart, and even though it's not always practical, I like that part of myself.

It's a challenge, trying to balance future-oriented fantasies with present-centered reality. The balance gets tipped for me when I focus too much on a future goal, and I end up worrying or stressing over it in the present. Suddenly, I see impending doom in my future, and I'm irritable and anxious and sometimes downright miserable in the present. And yes, I can be a bit dramatic, in case you haven't noticed.

At those times, I benefit from a gentle reminder either from a loved one, or from within me, to just be in the moment, because there's no point in worrying about the future right now. And then I'm back in balance, grounded, grateful for the reminder.

For better or worse, I tend to share the value of balancing present and future with those around me. During my son's early years, when I would see him giving minimal effort at school, or getting sucked into video or phone games for hours on end, it would drive me crazy and really upset me. But, I very rarely yelled or gave him time-outs. Nope, he got lectured, poor kid. He probably would've preferred a shorter and harsher consequence, but I wanted him to learn something.

My favorite and most polished lecture, I lovingly titled, "You only get this one life." I won't subject you to my lecture in its entirety, although it sure is perfected after all these years. Here's the gist: Think about the choices you are making for yourself and your life right now. Are they adding value to your life? Are they helping you to be a better person? Are you going to look back and regret this? You will not get to live this day or this time in your life over again. You only get this one life. Are you satisfied with how you're living it?

I wanted my son to participate fully in his life, to recognize the value and importance of this moment and the impact that his present choices have on his future. I wanted him to find meaning in doing his best at school and being fully present and engaged in his life. I didn't want him to look back with regrets, noticing how time flew by and how he missed out on some potentially amazing opportunities. I'm sure every parent wants the same for their children, and we do the best we can to help our kids "get it." The good news is, at sixteen, my son is starting to get it.

I also want the same thing for you. I want YOU to be present and engaged in your life right now, while looking towards the future and dreaming big. I want you to have the best life, a life you maybe thought wasn't possible. I want all your dreams to come true.

So how do you do that? How do you live fully in the moment, appreciating the "one life" you're given, while still looking towards the future? How can you find the right balance between today and tomorrow?

TAKE A RISK

Taking a risk requires you to be fully present, while looking towards the future. Taking a risk now can lead the way to reaching your dreams. Taking a risk is ideal for super motivated people, and it's also perfect for folks who are stuck in a rut, feeling unmotivated, and perhaps not really living for today or tomorrow.

A while ago, I was feeling ambivalent about my life. There were no major problems, but I just wasn't feeling motivated or excited about my circumstances, job, daily routine, or where my life was heading. I wasn't really grounded in the present, because I was bored, and I wasn't really looking towards the future because I was indifferent. I needed a challenge, something new, to keep me fresh, motivated, and active in my own life. You know what I did? I took a risk, and I started writing this book. I've never written anything outside of school papers, and I've never kept a journal for more than a week or two, so what made me think I could write a book?

Being completely honest, I didn't just decide one day to take a risk and then immediately start writing. I argued with myself, said I wasn't a writer, that I couldn't take on something as big as writing and publishing a book, that people wouldn't buy my book, and that I didn't even know if I could produce enough words to fill a book. But even while I was trying to talk myself out of it, I knew deep down that I was going to give it a shot. And I had butterflies in my stomach.

Be prepared, butterflies in the stomach happen when you are preparing to take a risk. If you're feeling a little anxious, then you are right on track! Taking a risk means you're doing something new, challenging yourself mentally or physically. Our bodies naturally go on alert, our senses are heightened, and we start feeling the butterflies. We are not actually in any danger, it just takes our bodies time to realize that everything is fine. Some people are uncomfortable with that feeling. Please, embrace the butterflies, take a risk, live your life.

So, back to my story about deciding to take a risk and write this book. Sure, I was nervous, and I worried that I might end up hating writing and dumping the whole project. But I figured I had nothing to lose besides the cost of a new laptop, and I needed a new laptop anyway. I also knew that there were important lessons and tips that I wanted to share with a broader audience, instead of just with one person at a time, so the potential gains were significant. I spent several days thinking it through, purchased a laptop, planned out when I was going write each day, and then I just went for it.

I never took a writing class, and I didn't spend even one minute researching how to be a good writer. That may seem like poor planning, or overly impulsive, but I had a feeling there was a TON of information out there, and I didn't want to feel overwhelmed or defeated before I even started. I deliberately chose to be naïve, and jumped right in. My goal was to enjoy the process, have fun, try something new, stretch my own limits, take a risk. I was grounded in the present during my writing time, while dreaming about the future and who my book might reach.

If you're feeling like your life is passing you by, you're stuck in a rut, going in circles, or you're just feeling ambivalent or unexcited about your day to day routine, take a risk. Remember, tomorrow is not promised to you, and you only get this one life…take a risk. What does that mean to you? How do you take a risk? If you're like me, Miss Safety, taking a risk might sound scary or impractical. Don't worry, you'll be fine.

If you haven't taken a risk in a long time, you may want to start small. Take a risk that is perfect for YOU, for YOUR life. The size of the risk doesn't matter, it's about being in the moment while looking towards the future, embracing what you're given, and living your life.

This may be "easy to say but hard to do," especially if you're not used to taking risks. But, it's important, and it's necessary if you really want to live your life. Here are some ideas to help get your creative, risk-taking juices flowing:

Try doing something you've never done before. Go somewhere you've never been, even if it's just ten minutes away from home. Research food from a different culture and then go taste the food at a new-to-you restaurant. Think about the things, the ideas and possibilities, that have bounced around in your head over the years, and you always pushed them aside because you weren't old enough, young enough, smart enough, brave enough, or maybe you didn't have the time or money. Entertain those thoughts now, and see if now is a better time, or if perhaps you can modify an old idea and make it the perfect thing for right now.

Apply for a promotion at your job, or even apply for a new job if you've been unfulfilled at your current job. Take on a side job that is different from what you've always done. Sign up for a dancing or acting lesson, make a new friend, go explore a new town, write a book! Get a new hairstyle or buy a shirt that is totally different from anything you've ever owned. Call an old friend you haven't spoken to in years and see what's going on with them. Take a train ride and make a random decision about where to get off. Take an online course or workshop. Go for a walk in the rain, then come inside and take a hot bath.

Brainstorm a range of possible risks, both large and small, and then choose a starting point that feels comfortable yet challenging and exciting to you. Make a plan and consider the possible outcomes, don't get too caught up in the details, and then follow through with it. Take a risk. And then take another risk.

To be clear, I'm not saying you should risk life and limb, or go broke, or do something that will place your health or safety in jeopardy. I'm saying to step out of your comfort zone. Embrace the health and resources you have today, and GO FOR IT. I'm willing to bet that you will never regret any risk you take. Clearly, most risks will not lead to fame and fortune, and some may end up just being learning experiences. That's okay, because that's not the point. You will grow, have more energy, and feel more engaged in your life and connected to yourself and the world, with each risk you take.

Maybe you feel limited by something, and taking a risk feels just too, well, risky for you. Perhaps you have a physical ailment or disability, or an emotional imbalance, or a substance abuse problem, or a chaotic home life, or you are in financial distress. I acknowledge the burden you are carrying, the toll it has taken on you, and the perceived comfort you may find in just being. And, I still want you to take a risk.

You can start with a less risky risk. Drive a different route to the store without looking up directions, pick up some books at the library on how to do a craft, learn how to draw by watching YouTube, ask a neighbor you don't know very well to share their favorite dessert recipe with you, check if there's a free workshop on photography at your local community college or library, challenge yourself to learn something about each continent. You can take a risk, and consequently live a fuller and more satisfying life, even if your current circumstances are challenging.

Do you remember my opening story about my dad passing away fifteen years ago? Speaking of taking risks, do you want to know how my mom is holding up? Well, she will turn sixty-seven next week, and as I'm writing this, she's packing her bags because she's flying to Guatemala tonight for a medical mission trip. She's already completed two medical mission trips to Haiti over the past couple of years. She also leads hikes, averaging nearly 30 miles most weeks. She completed a program last fall and is growing a small business. She regularly runs 5k races and half marathons, and she almost always medals in the top three in her age category. Did I mention that she will be 67-years-old next week? She's pretty incredible. She takes risks every single day, without having any guarantees. She's excited for her future, and she lives her life every day, fully engaged and present. She truly inspires me, and I hope she inspires you, too.

THINKING POINTS:

- Do you have balance in your life, between the past, present and future, or is this a challenge for you? Do you tend to get caught up in the future, or the past?

- When was the last time you took a risk? What was it?

- Is there something that is currently getting in the way or even stopping you from taking risks or trying something new?

ACTION ITEMS:

- Make a list of potential risks you can take. Think large and small, and see if you can include possibilities for different parts of your life – mental, physical, emotional, spiritual, etc. You can be as broad or as detailed as you like. Just let the ideas flow without judgment.

- Review your list and note which risks are perhaps too large for right now (in terms of time, costs, effort). If you have any risks on your list that are just too risky, go ahead and put a single line through them. No need to scribble them out, because who knows, you may want to come back to them later.

- Decide if you want to focus all of your energy on one larger risk, or if you'd rather make plans to do several smaller risks.

- Select the risk(s) you want to take first, finalize your plans, and go for it!

- Make sure you track your progress as you start taking risks. Check in with yourself regularly and notice how you're feeling about your life, circumstances, routines. Are you taking risks that keep you grounded in the present and excited for what's to come? Continue taking risks throughout your life. You may end up surprising yourself!

PRACTICE HARD

I STARTED PLAYING PIANO WHEN I WAS 3 years old. My piano teacher wouldn't enroll me until I turned 4, so my mom began my lessons when I was 3 ½. I practiced almost every day of my young life, through elementary school, junior high, and high school. There were some days when I didn't feel like practicing, and I would just bang on the keys and sigh loudly. However, I did not like feeling embarrassed, and that's what would happen when I showed up for a lesson without knowing the songs. So I practiced.

I remember practicing before, during and after classes in high school, and then putting in more time at home. The first few times I played a new piece, I usually went very slow, sometimes using only one hand at a time while getting used to the flow. I would then pick up the pace, and learn a few measures at a time, until I eventually learned the whole song. I would play each piece endlessly, even if (or especially if) I didn't care for it. I may have had some natural talent, but probably not more than the average person. So I worked hard.

Doing a good job, my very best, was something I valued, even if I was never going to perform the song in front of an audience.

I learned so much from playing piano, beyond how to actually play an instrument. The main lesson was NOT 'practice makes perfect' (because what is perfect anyway, and who actually wants to be perfect), but 'you perform how you practice'. If you are sloppy and distracted and counting the minutes when you are practicing something (an instrument, a sport, a new skill), you will likely not do so good when it counts (at a lesson, performance, game). You may even give up and feel defeated because you think it's too hard or you're just not good enough. But, if you set aside dedicated time each day to really focus on what you want to learn, really commit yourself to it, you will excel and create something you are proud of (even if you weren't born with a ton of natural talent in that area).

At my high school graduation, I gave a speech that summarized these ideas, called, you guessed it, "You Perform How You Practice." I was very quiet and shy in high school, and the thought of giving a speech to my entire class plus their families terrified me. But, sharing my message with my classmates was important to me. If you want to succeed at something, anything, you need to put in the work. Practice it over and over, even when it's hard and you're tired, even when you don't feel like doing it and you're bored or just over it, even when you'd rather be hanging out with friends and relaxing in front of the television. When you put in the time, the pay-offs are great.

During college, when I was learning how to be a social worker and psychotherapist, I was quite anxious. What if I said the wrong thing? What if I crossed my arms when I was supposed to lean forward and nod? What if I couldn't find the right balance of being supportive yet challenging? For a 20-year-old, that was a lot of pressure. So you know what I did? I practiced. A lot.

I listened and talked to my friends, sometimes formally when they knew I was practicing, and sometimes informally. I talked to strangers and practiced having "open" body language to quickly build trust and rapport in a conversation. I became a resident assistant (i.e., hall manager) in my dorm at college, and the students on my floor, especially the younger ones who were newly living away from home, would come and talk to me about their problems and concerns.

I practiced and practiced and I got hired at an entry level social work position while I was still in college. Getting a job was certainly not the end of my practicing…it was really just the beginning because then I had the opportunity to start honing my skills with 'real' clients. To this day, I still practice being a psychotherapist. Learning a new treatment or skill takes time, dedication, and commitment, and just like when I was learning to play piano, and learning the basics of being a social worker, I still need to put in the practice time.

I was never a piano prodigy by any stretch of the imagination. While I played at piano recitals, school talent shows, and in my school musical organizations, I was never one of those gifted children that could sit down and play a whole concerto after hearing it once. Not even close. But I was a hard worker, and I showed up every day. Practicing did not make my songs perfect, and that's not the point. The point is that if you make a commitment to yourself, to learn something by practicing it and rehearsing the heck out of it, you will find success.

PRACTICE HARD

There are several ways to practice hard. For starters, you can actually practice your skill, sport, instrument, hobby, or interest. (I bet you didn't see that one coming). Put in the time every day. Don't watch the clock or focus on how hungry, tired, or unmotivated you feel (on the hard days). Just show up, give it all you've got, and go home.

Another way to practice hard is to use visualization. If you're not familiar with visualization, please take your time with this section, because visualization is a powerful tool that can change your life. Visualization is NOT thinking positively about your life or circumstances, or even about focusing on getting the perfect outcome. You do need to have your ideal outcome in mind, but to use visualization in a way that will get you the results you want, you need to start at the beginning of the process.

Professional athletes use visualization all the time, because it works. Let's look at how an elite diver might use visualization. A diver arrives at practice and changes into her bathing suit. She sits on a bench in the locker room and closes her eyes. In her mind's eye, she sees herself walking out of the locker room and into the pool area. The bleachers are full of cheering fans, but she hears nothing. She sees the diving platform at the end of the pool, and she walks toward it with confidence. She feels strong, limber, comfortable, excited to show herself and the world what she's made of.

She sees herself climbing up the ladder to the platform, feeling confident and well-prepared. She feels the oxygen filling her lungs, and smells the scents of the pool. She arrives at the top, feels the texture of the platform beneath her, and she pauses to take a breath and make sure she's centered. She is focused and ready. Nothing can distract her. She takes off, exits the platform, feels herself going through the motions of twisting and flipping, then enters the water gracefully and with no splash. She resurfaces, swims to the side of the pool, and looks up to see her best score ever. That was amazing! The crowd is on their feet!

This all happens before the diver ever leaves the locker room. She's also going through this same visualization exercise before she gets out of bed each morning and prior to falling asleep at night. Every dive, every technique, every little detail, is practiced outside of the pool area as much as inside. Every twist, turn, flip and even the tiniest movement is played out in her mind countless times outside of the water, until it is perfected.

Professional baseball players do the same thing, as do skiers, gymnasts, and track and field stars. Performers, singers, dancers, comedians, talk show hosts…they use it too. The actors starring in your favorite action movie, they didn't just go out there and shoot the scene. They took the time to think it through carefully, to visualize each movement, and in their minds they could see, hear, touch, taste, and smell everything in the scene long before it happened.

There's an additional benefit to using visualization. It's not only a way to prepare and perfect a technique, it's also a way to keep you safe. Nerves and anxiety can really get in the way of performing at our best, and visualization is the best way to address those issues. If you repeatedly see yourself as calm and confident during your visualization sessions, you will be calm and confident when you are performing.

Let's go back for a second to my history as a pianist. Nobody formally taught me how to fully use visualization, however, when I was practicing at home, I was picturing myself performing either at church or school or wherever I was going to be playing in front of people. I saw myself being calm, confident, focused. In my mind, I sailed through each song, including the parts that had caused me to stumble during practice. In my mind, I was amazing, and that helped me to be a better player.

I'd like you to see the difference between not visualizing and then visualizing an activity. First, go outside, right now if you can, and take a walk around the block. If that's not possible, do a short physical activity wherever you are. Right now… Yes, now! Put down this book and go take a walk without reading further. I'll wait here for you.

Ok, welcome back! Now grab your companion workbook or journal and jot down how the walk was, and how you feel now.

Next, sit down and close your eyes. Take the next few minutes to visualize yourself doing the same activity. If you went for a walk, picture yourself stepping out the door and walking out to the sidewalk. You might do a couple quick stretches as you get started, or just shake out your arms and legs a bit. In your mind's eye, see yourself starting off down the sidewalk. You know the way, and you can picture the route. Notice your confident and tall posture, your tight core, your low shoulders and loose neck, your hands swinging freely by your sides. You are bright-eyed, alert, looking around with a pleasant and confident expression on your face. You feel yourself warming up pretty quickly because you are walking at a decent pace. You breathe in the fresh air, say hi to a dog who wanted to sniff you, and you decide to pick up the pace a bit more. You continue like this, and quickly you are circling back to where you started. You feel great, accomplished, like you want to smile or laugh because you feel so good. Now, are you ready to give it a shot? Visualize your own personal walk or activity, and then go and do it again. Please do not read further until you do you activity a second time. Think of this as a fun experiment!

When you return, grab your workbook or journal again, and note how your walk was and how you are feeling now. Did you notice any differences between your first impulsive walk and your second walk that you visualized in advance? Try this activity again in another area of your life, maybe later on today. Do the same activity twice, the first time just jumping right in and the second time visualizing the activity first. There is no denying the mind-body connection, and I really want you to take advantage of this powerful tool.

Another way to practice hard is to tell yourself to "run past the finish line," or "finish strong." I think of these phrases literally and figuratively. When you are learning something, or practicing a skill, no matter how tired you are, give your 110% at the very end of the practice session. This may sound easy, but I think we can all relate to how hard it really is.

Recently, I started running. Well, first I started walking, and then I added short "boosts" of running (as detailed in Day 2). Going through this process, I eventually learned how beneficial it was to sprint to the finish, but it took me a while to get to that point. Initially during my walks, upon seeing a speed bump or stop sign up ahead, I'd tell myself to GO, and then I'd take off at a good pace…and then slow to a walk a few feet before the mini-finish line. What was that about? I knew it was all in my head, and I felt frustrated and discouraged.

Have you ever done that? Given something your all only to peter out right before you cross the finish line? I'm sure we've all done it at some point. At school, work, in a sport or hobby…I'm guessing we can all probably give several examples of times we didn't finish strong or run past the finish line. So frustrating!

Set your sights on running past the finish line. Even if you aim to reach your goal on Sunday, plan to continue your routine through the following Wednesday. If you need to lose weight, aim for 5 pounds under the weight your doctor set for you. If you set a budget, stick with it for several months even after your bills are paid off. Practice hard.

Luckily, I worked through my mental roadblock of slowing down just short of my running targets, and I immediately starting feeling so much better. Even if I'm tired and out of breath, I am out there literally running past my mini-finish lines and finishing strong. If you hit a roadblock and feel like you can't finish strong, picture me beside you, running past your finish line with you. You got this!

Make a decision to practice hard, to practice as if you are performing. Visualize your ideal routines outside of practice to really hone your skills and boost your motivation. To live your best life, run past the finish line, finish strong, and you will have results that you are proud of.

THINKING POINTS:

- Is there a sport or skill, or perhaps a hobby that you want to learn or that you have been working on? How much effort have you been putting in?

- Are you satisfied with the progress you're making? Do you want to do better?

ACTION ITEMS:

- Set aside a specific amount of time each day to practice your skill, even just 15 minutes. Set a timer if you feel like you'll be distracted by watching the clock. Make this a priority, and plan your time in advance to take any schedule changes into account. For example, if you have a commitment on Wednesday evening, plan your practice time for Wednesday morning, even if it means getting up earlier.

- Make sure you have minimal or no distractions during your practice time. (Leave your phone in another room if possible). Remind yourself that this time is your designated practice time, and everything else can wait.

- Be comfortable and dress for the part. Practice hard!

- Practice visualization of your skill, as described in this chapter, before you get out of bed in the morning. Set your alarm for 10 minutes earlier to give yourself enough time without having to rush. Do this every single morning. Do it again every single night.

- Track your visualization times in your workbook or journal, and note how your actual practices improve. Are you making improvements, giving your all, doing better than ever before?

TAKE GOOD CARE OF YOURSELF

DID YOU EVER HAVE A DAY WHERE NOTHING seemed to be going in your favor? Where you hit snooze twice and still felt exhausted, you were out of your go-to breakfast food, traffic was extraordinarily heavy, your computer upgraded overnight and you couldn't even find your email program, there were ten new voicemails waiting to be heard, the air conditioning broke and your office feels like a sauna, and, oh shoot, is that allergies or a cold coming on?

That's actually how my day started last Friday, so welcome to my world. I thought Fridays were supposed to be "light," "casual," and even "fun." Isn't it really Saturday Eve, a time to dress down and talk about weekend plans? I guess I missed the memo.

Being completely honest, last Friday was not that unusual. Luckily, I don't typically wake up feeling exhausted, and I rarely run out of bananas (my usual breakfast). And, thank goodness we only get the major computer upgrades every few years, because I couldn't handle that any more often. But the heavy traffic, full workload, broken air conditioning, and questionable allergies are par for the course in my life. Can you relate?

I moved from Pennsylvania to California in 2009 to complete my doctoral dissertation. I started a full-time job that was much harder than I had anticipated, and then I needed to work on my dissertation research during the evenings and weekends. Plus, I was a single mom of an 8-year-old at the time, and I had to get him adjusted to a new coast, new school, new afterschool program, and to being away from his family and friends.

When I first started working at my new job, I stayed late or came in early whenever I could. My to-do list was never caught up, and there were always more emails and more stuff that needed done.

I was chronically tired, irritable, never exercised or felt like I had any time or energy, and I was pretty miserable. I thought that was just going to be my new normal. And then, after about ten months, I started having pain and tightness in my chest that came and went throughout the day for several days. I was well-aware of how stress can accumulate in the body; it was something I educated my clients on all the time. But I thought I was invincible, that I could continue pushing myself to the limits without breaking. When the chest pains started, I knew I needed to take care of myself quickly.

I contacted my supervisor and requested leave for the entire next week. I rescheduled my clients and arranged for coverage. I made hotel reservations in Santa Cruz, CA, just forty minutes away from where we lived. I got home, told my son we were taking a vacation, and we packed up our bags and bikes and left a few days later. That was seven years ago, and I clearly remember that vacation.

My memory can often be spotty, but I still remember everything we did that week…sitting on the beach, hiking in the redwood forest, riding the train through town, getting up early to ride our bikes to the wharf to see the sea lions and get breakfast, my son wanting to stay in the hotel room and watch kids' cable networks because we didn't have cable at home. It was a special time, my first vacation with my son since moving to California, and the first break I took from my new job.

When I returned to work the following week, I felt refreshed, renewed, and ready to resume my job. While on vacation, I had done quite a bit of thinking about my life and how I was going to manage everything. It had finally hit me that I was living on a different side of the country, was a single mom with a now 9-year-old, didn't have local friends or support, was working at a new and very challenging job, plus I was trying to complete my doctoral dissertation, the whole reason for being there in the first place.

That week away, I finally stopped and gave myself credit for everything I was doing, and acknowledged that maybe I was pushing myself a bit too hard. I loved spending time with my son that week, and I realized that I didn't have much quality time with him at home because I was just too busy and stressed out all the time.

I started making changes immediately, as soon as we returned from our impromptu vacation. To begin with, I no longer stayed late or started early at work. If there was an emergency or very urgent situation with a client that arose at the end of the day, I dealt with it quickly and requested overtime pay for the extra time I put in. I also prioritized my lunch break each day, and either took a walk, ate at a table away from my desk, or used the time to get caught up on personal emails.

After making some changes, I began noticing that I had more energy outside of work. I was in a better mood at home, and my son and I started playing "tourist" one day every weekend, where we could go and visit new places around the Bay Area. I was able to make real progress on my dissertation and graduated exactly one year later. I started connecting with others and finally nurtured my own needs for support and friendship. I learned an invaluable lesson.

TAKE GOOD CARE OF YOURSELF

I had been putting an incredible amount of pressure on myself, to do everything and meet everyone else's needs. That wasn't sustainable for me, and it's probably not sustainable for anyone. That stress, that pressure, builds up in our bodies and leads to things like anxiety, depression, weight gain, insomnia, digestive issues, irritability, eye twitches, neck and jaw pain...the list goes on and on.

If we don't take good care of ourselves, we end up feeling miserable and causing more harm than good to everyone around us. Has that ever happened to you? Have you ever stopped putting yourself first, or maybe you've never put yourself first, and now you're paying the price?

It's common to NOT take good care of yourself. There's a lot of pressure to be the best employee, the best parent, the best spouse, the best friend or colleague, to have a perfect home, maintain the best social media accounts, and somehow do everything while keeping a smile on your face. From my personal experience, and what I've learned from my clients, is that there's only one way to truly and authentically be the best worker, spouse, parent, etc., that you can possibly be. Take good care of yourself. When you put yourself and your needs first, not only do you feel better, but everyone around you benefits.

Do you remember how my day started last Friday? When it seemed like everything was falling apart? Well, it would have gone much differently and likely carried over into the weekend if I wasn't taking good care of myself every day. If I hadn't been putting myself first, I probably would have stayed late to get everything done in my sweltering office, picked up take-out on the way home, been cranky with my family Friday night, slept poorly, and then woke up feeling irritable and ill on Saturday morning.

Thankfully, what happened instead was I left my office several times throughout the day to get a few minutes of sunlight and fresh air. I got a reasonable amount of work done and handled everything that was pressing. I had a light snack in the afternoon, left work on time, thought about my evening and weekend plans while driving home, made a light and healthy dinner, and had a pleasant evening with my family that ended with me soaking in a milk bath and reading my Kindle. I woke up early the next morning, and happily started my weekend with quiet time writing and going for a walk. Take good care of yourself.

I've spent time getting to know myself over the past several years, finding out what really makes me happy and brings me peace and joy. For example, I've learned that soaking in a bath works wonders for me, and I'm known in my house for taking baths that last at least an hour, several times a week. I personally love soaking in milk baths. If you've never taken a milk bath, you have to try it! I make my own, and it includes Epsom salt and Dead Sea salt (to help with sleep, stress and muscle tension), powdered milk, cornstarch and baking soda (all to make the skin super soft and silky), and essential oil (I prefer lavender or jasmine). Pure heaven. I keep a large Mason jar filled with milk bath beside my tub, along with a little wooden scoop, and I honestly get happy just looking at it. (If you want my recipe, please visit www.restorebodyandsoul.com/books, or you can purchase a Mason jar of milk bath, handmade by me, at www.restorebodyandsoul.com/products).

Taking good care of yourself means making healthy lifestyle choices, and nourishing your whole self, including body, mind and spirit. One thing to keep in mind, is that taking good care of yourself doesn't always involve activities that you necessarily love, or that you initially enjoy. For example, exercising isn't something that most people love. We do it to keep our bodies healthy and strong, to keep our weight in check, and to be strong and fit across our years. Love it or hate it, regular exercise is part of taking good care of yourself.

Having a reasonable diet is also important. I've learned that if I take good care of myself and eat light, healthy meals, then I'm able to include some sweets here and there without any major issues. Being a lifelong vegetarian, I'm happy with a salad and vegetables, but I enjoy having something sweet at the end of a meal. Having a slice of cake or an entire dessert isn't a good choice for me, because my weight, digestive track, mind, and overall health pay the price. Instead, if I'm at a restaurant, I'll share a dessert and only eat a few (small) bites.

I enjoy watching the Food Network, and one time some food judges were being interviewed about what it's like to judge food. One judge was asked how she stays thin, when her job involves eating so much food. She replied that she always eats just three bites of any dish. The first bite gives instant pleasure, the second bite is very satisfying, and the third bite brings closure and contentment. After three bites, she said your taste buds and pleasure centers don't have the same reaction. I tried it, and I think she's absolutely right. Three bites of dessert is perfect. Try it and see what you think!

How can you take good care of yourself? Are you currently doing things each day to nurture yourself, or is this an area that could be improved upon in your life? Are you eating healthy foods and getting enough physical activity? What helps you to relax and lowers your stress? Do you feel good when you soak your feet after standing all day? Do you like taking a walk and listening to music, or soaking in the bathtub while reading your Kindle? What are some things you enjoy doing that are easily accessible, free or low cost, and can be done regularly?

Try adding small bursts of self-care throughout each day, such as going outside and either walking for 10 minutes or just taking 5 deep breaths with your face towards the sun. Slowly stretch your arms wide to open your chest while breathing deeply, then gently turn your head from side to side a few times. Use the restroom as soon as the urge strikes instead of waiting until it's urgent. Eat light snacks, such as small servings of grapes, cheese cubes, and pretzel sticks, to hold you over instead of feeling starved by mealtimes. Keep tennis balls or small rubber balls by your desk, so you can roll your feet on them a few times a day. Keep lotion nearby, so you can take literally 30 seconds and give yourself a short hand massage while moisturizing your skin.

I completely understand how hectic your days likely are, especially if they're anything like mine. And, you can still take good care of yourself, if you make it a priority. Small moments during the day can make a huge difference in how the rest of your day and evening go, and in how you perceive your day overall. Even the most stressful day can be managed, if you know what you need and make sure you take good care of yourself.

THINKING POINTS:

- Do you think it's important to take good care of yourself? Important enough to make it a priority?

- What do you currently do to nurture and care for yourself?

- Do you watch what you eat and make sure you get enough physical activity each day?

- Start thinking of free or low-cost, readily accessible activities that could be done regularly and often that make you happy, bring you peace, and calm your spirit.

- In your mind, review how your day went yesterday, or today if it's currently evening-time for you. Are there brief self-care moments you could have squeezed into your busy day?

ACTION ITEMS:

- Make a list of activities you enjoy, and include things you can do daily, weekly, monthly, and yearly.

- Pick a few of the activities from your daily list that you want to include in your day either today or tomorrow. You can choose several brief, self-care moments (e.g., light snack, deep breaths, lotioning your hands), and 1-2 activities that take longer (e.g., taking a walk, attending a yoga class, riding your bike, soaking in a bath). Think about each one and plan accordingly. At the end of the day, be sure to take time to reflect on how you felt throughout the day, and how you perceive your overall day.

- Pick a couple things from your weekly list, and figure out how you can incorporate them into your schedule. You may not want to do each one every week, but get out your calendar and see where you can fit them in.

- From your yearly list, and you may be merely fantasizing at this point, but can you pick one thing you'd like to do this year? Maybe there's a place you'd like to visit or a vacation you've been putting off because you're too busy? Add it to your calendar and just leave it there for now. That activity may or may not change as you get closer to the date, but just having something like that on your calendar will help you start thinking about the possibilities.

- Take a look at your diet. Are there tweaks you could make, in an effort to take good care of yourself? Perhaps you can switch out some unhealthy foods for healthy alternatives, or have smaller portions? If you need guidance in this area, please consider contacting a nutritionist.

- Be sure you're getting enough physical activity. If you're not currently taking good care of yourself in this area, you may want to consider contacting your doctor or a reputable personal trainer. Getting your body moving is non-negotiable when it comes to taking good care of yourself, so talk to a professional if necessary, and get moving.

CONCLUSION

YOU MADE IT! DID YOU READ THROUGH ALL fourteen days? Did you connect strongly with some of the tips, perhaps less with others? Once you complete the entire book, it may be helpful to go back and select a chapter, and really focus on that one lesson. Once you can consistently apply it to your life, then continue on and dig into another chapter.

I want to remind you that this book is not about finding happiness, that mythical experience that is so fleeting that I wonder if it truly exists. You may have found moments of happiness as you applied some of the lessons, and that's wonderful. But, when the "high" fades, as all extreme feelings do, please carry on with what you learned, knowing that what you're doing is creating a life that is meaningful, a life that will continue to bring you satisfaction and contentment across your years. That is what is truly important.

You may feel completely satisfied after applying only a few lessons to your life, and that's great if that happens. Your life may not be perfect, because who has the perfect life anyway, but you could easily feel significantly better after consistently utilizing even just a handful of tips. At that point, I encourage you to press on, to dive wholeheartedly into another lesson. There's so much more to receive, and I don't want you to miss out on anything.

When you're all finished with this book, or you're at least done with it for the time being, take out your companion workbook and turn to the end. At this point, your workbook should be well-worn and hopefully much loved.

Right now, think about how you're feeling about your life, situation, circumstances, your overall "life satisfaction." On a scale of 1-10, with 1 being "my life is in the toilet right now" and 10 being "my life is AMAZING and I'm completely satisfied," what number would you give your life? Please don't rush through this. Take your time and think about how you feel about your life when you wake up in the morning, and when you're getting ready for bed at night. Think about your daily and weekly routines and how you spend your time. How satisfied are you? Write it down.

Now, flip back to the first page of your companion workbook, where you answered the same question before you started on this journey. Is there a difference in the number? Did your "life satisfaction" score increase over the course of this journey? How do you feel about your before and after ratings?

But wait, we are not done yet. I really hope you learned some things about yourself over the course of this book. I hope you experienced growth, gained insight into what it means to live your life, and most of all had a little fun with the process. In case you didn't quite get enough, I'm excited to share one more insight with you.

As I was writing this book, I was continually reminded of how simple and accessible these fourteen tips are, for everyone. Now, don't misunderstand me here. I think many of them are "easy to say, hard to do," and I completely appreciate the effort it takes to apply each lesson because I had to learn them all myself. Believe me, I am right there with you. And yet, all of the skills needed are within your reach, just waiting for you.

YOU ALREADY HAVE EVERYTHING YOU NEED

You already have what you need inside of you to live your life, to be the best you, to have the life you always dreamed of. It's been there all along, and maybe you just didn't realize it, or maybe you needed some reminders. You were born perfect, whole, not lacking in any way, and no matter what you may have grown up believing or what you may be telling yourself sometimes even now, you are special, valuable, and absolutely priceless.

This is your time. You may still be working on mastering and internalizing some of the lessons from this book, and that's totally fine. You are on the right path, and that's what matters. Some lessons may take months or even years of practice. We all have different journeys, and you are exactly where you're supposed to be. Just keep putting one foot in front of the other, and your life will keep getting better. At times, you may still feel uncomfortable, vulnerable, and maybe even a little afraid. All of that is totally normal, and it's expected, and it's okay. Just don't stop. Remember, trust the process.

I suggest keeping this book handy for the future, in case you find yourself in a period of ambivalence or stagnation and you need some reminders of what to do. Or, somewhere along the line, you might need some ideas on how to lower your stress or increase your motivation. Honestly, I still struggle with some of these concepts, and even I use this material as a reference when needed.

If you are struggling to apply any of the tips, I welcome you to schedule a consultation appointment with me, or perhaps consider reaching out to a local therapist or counselor in your community for extra support and guidance. If you want to dig deeper and learn some additional skills for the body and mind, you can check my website for opportunities to attend my workshops and classes, online or in person.

Thank you for reading my book. I hope you enjoyed reading it and applying the lessons, as much as I enjoyed writing it. As I wrote each chapter, I was reminded of the power behind these simple lessons, and I also realized that I had stopped applying some of the lessons to my own life along the way. So really, I wrote this book for all of us. We are each a work in progress, on our own unique journeys through life, and we all need reminders and guidance along the way.

I would love to hear about how you've grown and changed over the course of this book. Please share your story with me at www.restorebodyandsoul.com/ContactMe.

If you enjoyed this book, the best compliment you can give me, as a new author, is an honest review on Amazon. And, if you have any ideas for me for future books, please Contact Me and let me know!

ABOUT THE AUTHOR

Ann LeFevre is a PhD, Licensed Clinical Social Worker, and has been a practicing psychotherapist since 2002. Dr. LeFevre is also a Certified Massage Therapist and a Certified Acupressurist. She created Restore Body and Soul, a holistic wellness enterprise that integrates Eastern and Western philosophies, and is centered on the mind-body connection. At Restore Body and Soul, clients can access evidence-based psychotherapy, massage therapy, professional and personal consultation, and workshops and classes on acupressure and other wellness topics. They can also purchase soothing, hand-blended bath and body products designed to ease stress, restore energy, and enhance sleep and relaxation.

Dr. LeFevre realized during childhood that her purpose in life is to help others live their best lives, using the resources they have within them and available to them. *Life Your Life: 14 Days to the Best You* is Dr. LeFevre's first book, and is a compilation of lessons and tips that have helped her clients over the years to become unstuck and move forward in their lives, to ease stress and be present in their lives, and to truly live their best lives. Illustrated with stories from her own life, Dr. LeFevre hopes the lessons in *Live Your Life* will speak easily and authentically to readers, and she welcomes feedback and suggestions for future books.

67744889R00084

Made in the USA
San Bernardino, CA
27 January 2018